• HOME CLUB •

HOME CLUB

Up-and-Comers and Comebacks at Acme Comedy Company

PATRICK STRAIT

MINNESOTA HISTORICAL SOCIETY PRESS

mnhspress.org

The Minnesota Historical Society Press is a member of the Association of University Presses.

Manufactured in United States of America.

10 9 8 7 6 5 4 3 2 1

∞ The paper used in this publication meets the minimum requirements of the American National Standard for Information Sciences—Permanence for Printed Library Materials, ANSI Z39.48-1984.

International Standard Book Number
ISBN: 978-1-68134-316-7 (paperback)
ISBN: 978-1-68134-317-4 (e-book)

Library of Congress Control Number: 2024949140

CONTENTS

PREFACE

It's Sunday night at Acme Comedy Company, and the club is at an absolute fever pitch. This atmosphere is unusual, because the club isn't typically open on Sundays. But tonight is special. Tonight, some of the biggest names in comedy have joined together to share memories and catch up on stories from the road.

At one table, Chad Daniels is holding court with Greg Coleman and Tim Slagle. At another, Ryan Stout is chatting with Mike Earley. Just outside the bar, Jackie Kashian is laughing with Brandi Brown. And by the bathrooms, J. Elvis Weinstein is locked into a deep conversation with David Crowe. It's a who's who of Minnesota and Minnesota-adjacent comedy, cutting loose on familiar turf. The reason for this rare Sunday-night gathering is to celebrate the club's thirty-year anniversary. Since 1991, Acme has been a staple of Minneapolis's North Loop neighborhood, entertaining hundreds of thousands—if not millions—of comedy fans throughout its illustrious history.

To commemorate the occasion, the club has hosted a week's worth of all-star-caliber lineups, bringing together various generations of comics for something of a quasi–comedy festival. Aside from being hilarious (and at this particular party, good and drunk), all of these comics share a common bond: they all consider Acme their home club. In the comedy world, a home club is a sacred space where comedians first cut

Comics of different eras sign posters during Acme's thirty-year anniversary. *Courtesy Acme Comedy Company*

their teeth and find a sense of belonging in an art form that can be isolating and lonely. It's a place where comics of all levels of experience can work on new material, where wide-eyed up-and-comers and established headliners look to each other for inspiration and camaraderie. For the past three decades, countless homegrown comedians, along with comedy vagabonds, have called Acme their home club.

It's not just comedians at this party, either. Booking agents and managers have flown in from New York and Los Angeles to pay homage to the club. Former Acme staff are back to reminisce and share insane stories about hecklers, snowstorms, and bachelorette parties from hell. And inside the restaurant, there's one table of quiet Chinese people, taking in the boisterous spectacle happening all around them. But no matter who they are, how much fame they've achieved, or how far they've traveled to be here, one person among the crowd commands more attention and respect than anyone else.

Louis Lee has been the owner of Acme Comedy Company since the day it opened back in November 1991. He is the reason the club has survived and grown when so many other comedy clubs have fallen by the wayside. A Chinese immigrant, Lee looks less like a comedy kingpin and more like a local restaurant manager. Which makes sense, because at his core Lee is still the same hardworking busboy he was when he first moved to America in the early eighties. As the club gets rowdier, Lee remains his usual reserved self. He's dressed in a sport coat for the occasion, a break from his customary attire of a polo shirt and khakis. Lee wears his humility and humbleness on his sleeve. He smiles politely as one person after another stops by to offer well-wishes and pay their respects.

It would be easy (and deserved) for Lee to revel in the success of the club. But Lee isn't one to accept credit. He believes Acme exists for the comics first and foremost, a mentality that has endeared him to performers since the very beginning. Years ago, Lee decided to take down a small sign hanging from the stage that read "Acme Comedy Company" because he felt it took the focus off the performers. "When they're onstage, I want the comics to feel like the club belongs to them," Lee explains.

This night is different. Even as a litany of comedians hops onstage to perform for an intimate audience of their peers, Acme itself is the star attraction. Unlike a standard comedy show, where comics are doing battle-tested material, these sets have the energy of a celebration. It's like a bunch of souped-up wedding toasts, packed with inside jokes and targeted punch lines, and designed to get a reaction that would only work on this night, in this club, with this crowd. All the while, Lee stays in the back of the club, smiling but not showing too much emotion. He has the face of a man who has seen everything the

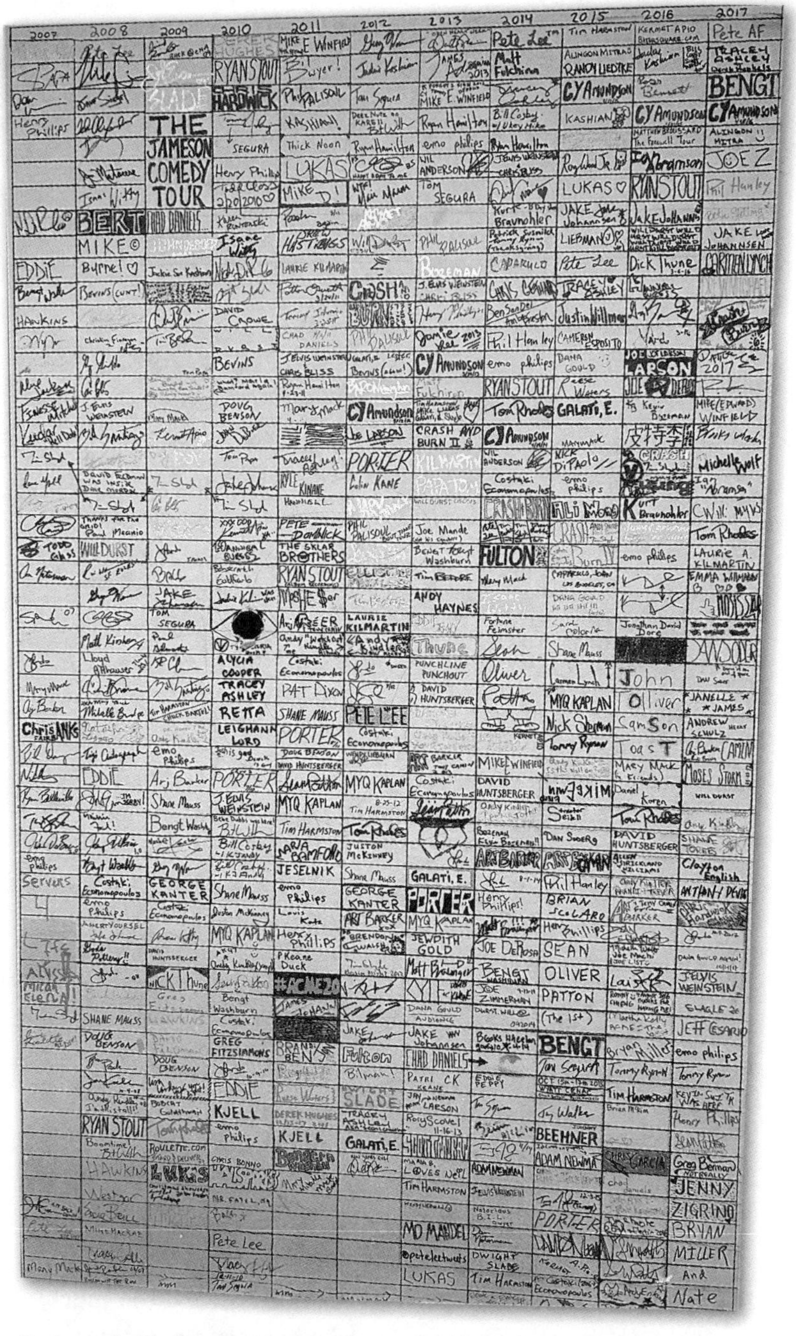

Each week, the headline act at Acme autographs the wall.
Courtesy Acme Comedy Company

comedy business has to throw at him, and lived to tell the tale. Whether it's J. Elvis Weinstein sharing a story about Lee pouring whiskey in coffee cups for him as a teenager, or Mike Earley making a crack about Louis's former partner-turned-comedy adversary Scott Hansen, Lee remains stoic.

Acme wasn't a success right out of the gate. Money problems, egos, competition, and controversy have all threatened the existence of the club over time. Just like the comedy industry itself, Acme and Lee have experienced peaks and valleys over the past several decades. But like the comics who consider Acme their home club, this place is Lee's home club as well. As a man who spent years trying to find his place in the world, Lee has always had the soul of a comedian. He's an outcast, a free spirit, an interrupter. A man who has succeeded where countless others have failed. And in this comedy club downstairs in the Itasca Building in Minneapolis, he's created a home for others just like him. If "home is where the heart is," then a lot of extremely funny hearts have made Acme Comedy Company home since the beginning.

Whether it was determined funny people for whom the club was a launching pad to comedy fame, nervous first timers looking to find common ground with others who share their same comic sensibilities, or battle-tested comedy veterans needing to go back to their roots, Acme has always brought people together and made them feel, well, like they're home. But just like any home, not everything always runs smoothly.

The comics themselves have been challenged in their relationships with the audience and with each other. Lee faced challenges from critics who said comedy was a dying art, and later from those who questioned how he chose to run his club. And all along the way, Lee found his biggest challenges coming from inside. Pride, guilt, joy, sadness, anger, and, naturally, laughs filled Lee's story, just as they filled the hallowed walls of Acme.

· CHAPTER 1 ·

BORN LOSER

Louis Lee was always the loser of his family. At least that's what he believes. The fifth of eight siblings, Lee was born in Hong Kong in 1958. As a child, Lee grew up in a lower income household, in an apartment with four bedrooms that housed ten people. His grandfather was a devout Catholic, and Lee and his siblings all attended Catholic school in Hong Kong. Lee was an altar boy, followed the rules, and got a job at a toy assembly factory at the age of fourteen to help support his family. Lee was a well-behaved, by-the-book Chinese boy who didn't cause any trouble. That is, until he turned sixteen. At that point, all bets were off. "On one hand you want to be a good Catholic boy," he says. "But on the other hand you're still a sixteen- or seventeen-year-old boy."

Lee wasn't doing anything out of the ordinary for kids his age—dating, sneaking around, getting into fairly innocent trouble—but his family still viewed him as the black sheep. Lee's father was a hardworking man who felt his potential was stymied by Chinese culture, and he didn't want to see his son waste his abilities. "My father is my grandfather's oldest son," Lee explains. "In the forties, he got accepted to the University of Hong Kong medical school. But my grandfather told him, 'No. You're not going. You come work for me at my sock factory.' Traditionally [in Chinese culture] you do what your

Louis Lee (right) as a baby. *Courtesy Louis Lee*

father says. He didn't have a choice. So he went to work for my grandfather." Later on, when Louis's father had children of his own, he held them to the same expectations and beliefs of the elder Lee, causing tension within the family. "My oldest brother didn't do well in school, and my father held it against him his whole life," Louis says.

Fortunately, Lee's sisters performed well in school, restoring some faith that the family would succeed. Unfortunately for Lee, though, much like his father he found himself beaten down by his grandfather's harsh judgment. "[My siblings and I] still joke about how I was grandfather's favorite grandkid until elementary school," he laughs, though a faint trace of shame lies in his tone. "Then I went from the favorite to one of the losers. He was very hard on me. We have a tradition where we all eat dinner together every night. So every night we'd sit down at the table, and my grandfather would just start to criticize everybody."

Louis Lee in his formidable teenage years. *Courtesy Louis Lee*

The alienating negativity Lee experienced from his grandfather, combined with his rebellious nature and somewhat lackadaisical attitude toward education, didn't bode well for Lee during his teenage years. "I just got worse once I started high school," he says. "And my parents, they didn't have a lot of money. So they had saved up enough for a few of us to go to college, and it wasn't going to be me. My parents decided not to invest in me." Instead, Lee's parents moved all of their children who were under the age of twenty-one from Hong Kong to the United States in search of more opportunities. In 1977, Lee and his siblings arrived in Minneapolis.

"Everyone got two hundred dollars," he recalls. "We lived in Cedar Square West, in a three-bedroom apartment for six or seven of us, which was illegal at the time. Our parents gave us a Buick Skylark, dropped us off, and went back to China." Unsure of what to do next, Lee enrolled in school at the University of Minnesota and pursued a degree in sociology. However, he admits that he really had no plans for what to do with that degree, other than getting his parents off his back. "I decided to get a liberal arts degree so that I could show my grandfather I wasn't totally worthless," Lee remembers. "My whole purpose of getting a degree was just to graduate and show him that I'm not a loser. After that, I really didn't give a shit what I did with it."

Lee knew he needed to pursue a more feasible path to help him make money and survive. He decided to get into the restaurant industry, which is where his real American education began. "I started at the Radisson Hotel," he recalls. "There were several different bars and restaurants there at the time. The two restaurants were the Flame Room, which was a big restaurant with a fireplace and orchestra. It was still very formal dining. Then there was another restaurant called the Lodge. My first job was working in those restaurants as a busboy."

Lee got the job at the Radisson after living in America for just two weeks. Three weeks after that, he was nearly fired. "I had just moved here and cannot speak the language very well," he explains. "I worked the lunch shift. And one morning the phone kept ringing while I was setting up the room. The host hasn't showed up, so no one is answering the phone. It keeps ringing, so I go and pick it up. It's someone making a reservation. I could barely understand what they were saying, so I wrote the person's last name down but I spelled it wrong. Anyways, that day was crazy busy. After lunch, the host comes up to me and says, 'Did you take a reservation? It was for a very important regular that we have.' And she smacked me in the back of the head. She says, 'You dumb chink.' I didn't even know what that meant at the time." Lee's manager decided to give him another chance. "The manager moved me from days to nights. So I stayed another month or two, and one night this new guy tells me that everyone is going to the bar next door, and says he'll give me a ride home after we have some drinks. That's how I first started to meet the hotel people."

Lee was searching for a sense of belonging. "The Chinese community in Minnesota was very small," Lee says. "People would find each other, and then every year when new people would arrive from Hong Kong everyone would get together. They would all speak the language, and had jobs that were Monday through Friday, so they had weekends off to get together with Hong Kong people." It would have been a no-brainer for Lee to join the Chinese community of Minnesota, but his work schedule didn't make that a viable option for developing a social life. "I would work nights when everyone would get together, so I could never go," he recalls. "So the restaurant people would become my community instead."

Soon, Lee found himself frequenting the bars on Seventh Street with colleagues from around the service industry, despite not speaking much English and not fully understanding some of the culture-defining social cues. "I got a job at the peanut bar in the Radisson called the Haberdashery, where everyone would throw peanut shells on the floor," he says. "And I think with the exception of me, my boss, and maybe one or two other people, everyone who worked there was gay. The first week I worked there, everyone kept asking me, 'Are you one of the brothers?' I had no idea what that meant. As soon as they all knew I wasn't gay, they quit hitting on me, but I was accepted into another subculture at that point." In the late seventies and early eighties, the gay community wasn't widely accepted, viewed by the larger community as something of a seedy sector of society and relegated to specific bars and restaurants and not welcomed into the mainstream establishments. For Lee, however, these folks were his friends. "I remember on my last day at the Haberdashery, all of my friends got together before my shift and took me to the Gay 90's," Lee recalls, referring to the legendary gay bar in Minneapolis. "They got me so drunk, and then we all went back to work. It was the best."

Even with a new social circle, Lee struggled to find a sense of purpose. That aimlessness, combined with his less-than-impressive college credentials and some challenging work run-ins, kept Lee feeling anxious and insecure. "To me, I'm thinking I'm just dumb," he recalls. "I'm not good in school. I'm not good at work. What do I have left?"

As had been the case since he arrived in America, Lee found a sliver of encouragement from his work colleagues. "My boss at the Haberdashery, he became my friend. And he told me that I was really good at what I did, and I just needed to keep going. When you start to have positive reinforcement, even as a busboy, that changes things." Soon after, Lee was named employee of the month at his job, as his work ethic and affable personality were revealed and began to get noticed. It wasn't long before he was offered the opportunity to move on to a new position.

"Other restaurants wanted to hire me," Lee says. "My manager says, 'Stay here and work for me, and in six months I'll make you a waiter.' So I agree. Then six months later, the manager tells his boss, 'We need to make Louis a waiter.' [His boss] looks at him and says, 'That fucker cannot speak English.'" Vulgarity aside, the boss had a point. Lee still couldn't speak much English. But the language barrier didn't stop him from finding other ways to acclimate to the local culture and local people. Especially when it came to his romantic life. "My junior and senior year I dated a Chinese girl," Lee remembers. "She was a year or two younger than me. Her mother came to visit after the first year she lived in America, and she didn't like me because I was a sociology major. How many boys in Hong Kong major in sociology? No one. So her mom took one look at me and was like, 'Not him.'"

Despite his professional success, Lee once again found his confidence snuffed out by the judgment of his own people. "At this point, my grandfather doesn't like me because I'm not typical. My girlfriend's mom doesn't like me because she thinks I'm a loser. My self-esteem was just hit really hard by all of it."

Lee decided the only way to prove himself in his new home would be to learn English. While he picked up plenty from his schoolwork and his time at the restaurant, he actively looked for more ways to expand his cultural knowledge and language skills. "I would go to the theater and watch one movie every week," he remembers. "Reading and writing in English was so much different than day-to-day conversation, so this was how I tried to learn."

After he and his girlfriend broke up, he began dating an American girl. She introduced him to another cultural and linguistic phenomenon, one that was exploding locally at that time, one that Lee had never heard of before. "In 1981 the girl I was dating told me, 'You're working really hard, and I know you want to fit in. I think there's something you should see.' She took me to see my very first stand-up comedy show." The show was the Minnesota Comedy All-Stars, comprised of local comedy standouts Louie Anderson, Alex Cole, Jeff Cesario, and Joel Madison. Stand-up had taken off over the past year or two, and the All-Stars had become the hottest ticket in town, regularly selling out shows at the Dudley Riggs' Experimental Theatre Company in the Seven Corners neighborhood of Minneapolis.

"I would only get half of the show, but the crowd was so good that I'd be like, *Wow. This is how people communicate with each other.* It was different from my textbooks and different than movies. Movies were scripted; here they just talked naturally." Soon, Lee found himself regularly hitting stand-up shows all over town, whether it was at Dudley Riggs' or Mickey Finn's or the Comedy Cabaret. He was hooked on the art. But he was also hooked on the community. "It was like five or six bucks to see a show," he recalls. "We went to see a lot of comedy because it was all people my age who would show up, drink a beer, and watch the show. To me, I was thinking, *This is how I can learn more English, and I can be funny when I talk to other people by stealing jokes from the comics.*"

The Minneapolis Comedy All-Stars (left to right: Jeff Cesario, Louie Anderson, Alex Cole, Joel Madison). *Courtesy Jeff Cesario*

After graduating college, Lee got a job at a Chinese restaurant off of Interstate 494 in Minneapolis called Mandarin Yen, where he found an opportunity to combine his restaurant experience with his newfound love of stand-up. "They hired me as a host, and moved me up to assistant manager," Lee recalls. "I spent the next four years there. At one point, I told the owner that he was spending too much on entertainment. Every bar on 494 had a Top 40 band, and he couldn't charge cover because no one else did. So I suggested he try stand-up comedy." With nothing to lose, Lee's boss gave him the OK to introduce comedy to the massive banquet space in the restaurant. Not sure where to turn, Lee reached out to the comedy kingpin of Minnesota, Scott Hansen, and invited him to take a look at the space. Hansen was impressed with the potential, and soon he was promoting comics at the restaurant nearly every weekend.

Though Lee's idea was proving to be a smart decision, the owner of the Mandarin Yen was still dissatisfied. Like many before him, he looked to Lee as his scapegoat. But Lee had grown. He'd developed a sense of confidence that allowed him to finally push back. "I knew I found something I was good at," Lee says proudly. "But the owner was mad because the money wasn't coming in fast enough. I remember one day he came in and he was just in a foul mood, and he snapped at me for having three busboys working instead of cutting someone loose. I heard that and thought, *Seriously? He's yelling at me, and I'm saving him a huge amount of money.* And he's still only paying me $14,000 a year, working seven days a week. So I decided that I didn't need this anymore and walked out."

Lee left with every intention of using his newfound sense of self-worth not only for his own betterment but for the betterment of others like him. "I felt like if I did really well in my job, whatever job that was, then the next Chinese person who applied for a job wouldn't have to go through as much as I did," he says. "My bosses would tell me that I was one of the best employees. And to them, I was one of the first Chinese people they had ever met. So deep down I'm thinking, *It's not about me; it's about the next person. Everyone will look at that person differently based on what I do.*"

Those words would foreshadow Lee's future as a stand-up comedy club manager and an advocate for developing and growing comedy and comics. But soon he learned that in business and in life, sometimes you need to have a complete breakdown before you get to experience a breakthrough.

· CHAPTER 2 ·

BROKEN SKULLS AND BROKEN PROMISES

In the 1980s, no person was more influential in Twin Cities comedy than Scott Hansen. One of the original pioneers of local comedy, Hansen started his career alongside names like Louie Anderson, Alex Cole, and Bill Bauer. His early success led him to branch out and open his own comedy club, Scott Hansen's Comedy Gallery (located inside J. R.'s Restaurant and Lounge in downtown Minneapolis). This stage was where the likes of Jerry Seinfeld and Jay Leno made their first Minnesota appearances and kick-started the local comedy boom, which Hansen supported both at his own club and at venues all around the city. Even after Lee left Mandarin Yen, Hansen continued to find success promoting comedy in that location, as well as new rooms, like William's Bar and others. Business was so good for Hansen, in fact, that he was starting to outgrow his current spaces and needed to think bigger if he was to keep up with the seemingly never-ending demand for comedy in the Twin Cities. But to realize his ever-expanding vision, he'd need help.

Meanwhile, Lee had taken a job across town as a waiter at a bar called Trumps in Seven Corners. A typical college bar, Trumps had been around for about four or five years, never

Minnesota stand-up comedy kingpin Scott Hansen. *Courtesy Scott Hansen*

turning much of a profit. The owner decided he needed to find someone who would partner with him and purchase a stake in Trumps. He called on the owner of a bar in the Riverside neighborhood of Minneapolis named Rick Janucz. Janucz agreed to run Trumps for six months, and if the venture proved successful, he would buy it. And just like that, Janucz became Lee's boss. The arrangement didn't last long. "[The owner] called me one day and told me, 'I don't like Rick Janucz; I don't like how he runs the place. He's out. Maybe you should try it,'" Lee recalls. "He said 'You've got four months to turn this around, and if you do it you can buy up to 51 percent of this place.' So I said, 'OK. I'll do it.'"

Lee hit the ground running and quickly implemented successful strategies at the struggling bar, proving his ability as a bar and restaurant manager to his boss and, more importantly, to himself. "This is the first time I got into management and had someone say, 'You can do whatever you want to get the number up,'" Lee continues. "Around this same time, I met a good friend named Jim Meyer. We were both bartending [at Trumps], and he had a lot of bar experience. So I told him that when I bought the place, he and I would be partners." The numbers stayed steady, and four months later Lee intended to follow through on the plan to purchase a majority stake in the bar. The owner, however, had other ideas. "He said, 'Let's wait a few more months and see if the numbers stay up.' So a few months later, numbers are still good, and I ask again. He tells me, 'No, not yet. I want you to tell me what you can do to make it bigger. How much money are you willing to put in for improvements and all of that.' So I asked how much he was thinking, and he said $50,000."

Not sure where to turn, Lee called on his brothers and sisters. He explained the opportunity and asked if they would loan him the money. They agreed, but even with the necessary funds, things weren't progressing the way they should have. "The owner kept stalling," he says. "And I was pissed." While this was going on, Janucz had returned to working at his restaurant in Riverplace and caught wind of the deal Lee was trying to put together. One night, he called Lee with a counterproposal. "Rick called me and said, 'Why don't you buy into my bar? I'm moving to Reno to open another bar, and I'll need someone to run this place.' He tells me he'll sell me 50 percent of the bar for $100,000. So I talked with Jim, and he said, 'Let's do it.'"

Lee went back to his family to ask for an even bigger loan. While his parents were already in their sixties, the family had seen his success in managing other people's restaurants and decided to put their faith in him to run his own. They allowed him to borrow against their life savings. "When Louis wanted to go into the restaurant and comedy business, we were very supportive and proud of him," says Louis's sister Catherine. "Our parents were very open and supportive to what we wanted to do, just as long as we didn't take drugs or do bad things, and that we were being a good person." With that, Lee was a partner in the restaurant, and he assumed it would be his to run for the foreseeable future. That future turned out to be much shorter than he anticipated.

"Two months later Rick comes back from Reno," Lee laughs. "So I'm like, now what? He says he can either buy me out with our cash flow over the next five years, or [we] can figure out a way to expand." Having tied his future to this venture, Lee decided on the latter. And he had just the idea for how to grow. "The second floor of Riverplace Plaza had been empty for years," Lee recalls. "The owners of the building had this great idea one summer. They said, 'Let's do summer theater.' They built a big stage and a really nice space, but the whole thing fell apart and just sat there. So I got the idea to do stand-up comedy there. And I knew just who to turn to." Once again, Lee called on Scott Hansen and invited him to take a look. The timing was ideal for Hansen, who saw the size of the space and the prime location and jumped at the opportunity. Soon, Hansen shuttered his operation in J. R.'s, and in the fall of 1987, Hansen, Lee, and Janucz became partners in the Comedy Gallery Riverplace.

Though on paper Lee was an owner in a comedy club venture, he had no involvement with the comedy side of the business. The deal was simple: Lee and Janucz would run the bar, and Hansen would manage the comedy and take the money from ticket sales. It worked. The 250-seat club quickly became a success. Names like Joel Hodgson, Ellen DeGeneres, and Dana Gould graced the club in its first few months, packing the house with patrons who were ready to drink, laugh, and spend money. "I did what I did best, which was run a restaurant," says Lee. "And Scott did what he did best, which was book and promote comedy. That place had been empty for four years, and now it's packed. The restaurant guys thought it was incredible. And in the back of my mind I'm thinking, *Louis, you've done it again*. I think everything I touch turns to gold."

Thanks to the Comedy Gallery, the landlord saw the potential of the space and decided to sell it to a company that wanted to turn it into a nightclub. However, he wasn't going to leave the trio out in the cold. "The building's owner offered to sell us the historic building that was in front of our space," Lee recalls. "It was a three-story building, and had a different layout than the Riverplace building. He told us that he thought the future was in brewpubs, and that we could build a brewery in the basement, have a restaurant on the main floor, and then turn the top into a comedy club. For Scott, it was either do this or lose his club six months in and go crawling back to J. R.'s, so we became partners in a brewpub." While the price tag was hefty, the partners made it work, and soon the new Comedy Gallery had eclipsed the success of its former location. "Business was booming," Lee recalls. "The money was coming in fast, but we still had huge debt."

A short time after the brewpub was up and running, Lee got an opportunity to replicate the success of the Riverplace venture at a location in Galtier Plaza in downtown St. Paul. Between his past successes running restaurants and maybe a bit of arrogance, Lee was confident the new location would be a no-brainer for him and his partners. Hansen, however, thought differently. "Scott said no way," Lee says. "He said we owed way too much money already. I said, 'Look, let's just go check it out and see what they have to say.'" The space was perfect, and the financial terms made sense. The partners would have to shoulder more debt, but Lee believed the reward was worth the risk. Reluctantly, Hansen and Janucz agreed, and soon Lee was negotiating a lease for a second Comedy Gallery location in Galtier Plaza.

Then one night, everything changed.

Money had become tight at Riverplace, to the point that Lee wasn't cashing his paychecks. Soon, he had accumulated upward of $15,000 in unclaimed salary. "We needed money to cover payroll," he says. "So I called my personal banker and said I needed him to float me the money to cover payroll, and that I would give him the paychecks to borrow against. He agreed, and told me to drive up to North Branch and he'd take care of it."

Lee decided to make the trip on, of all days, Halloween 1988. During the drive, a truck pushed Lee's car off the road, causing a catastrophic accident that shattered Lee's skull. He was rushed to the hospital, where doctors were less than optimistic about his chances of survival. "They called my business partners and said I had a serious head injury," Lee says plainly. "And that they should call my family because I probably wasn't going to make it much longer." Hansen and Janucz panicked. The pressure of taking on the financial burden of two locations was already daunting, and losing Lee would saddle them with even more debt. "[Scott] was thinking he already owes $800,000, and now Louis has me in for another $800,000. And now he might be a vegetable. So if he dies, what the hell do I do?"

Not only did Lee survive the accident, but doctors were able to piece his skull back together, leaving him with no brain damage whatsoever. Lee returned to work fairly soon after, despite slowed speech and a partially paralyzed face that would take many years to heal. Lee remained adamant about seeing his vision for the club through to completion. Hansen and Janucz decided to lean on Lee for additional money for the business. "Right after New Year's, Scott came to me and said we needed another $150,000 to show the Port Authority on the St. Paul project," Lee recalls. "So I called my mom in Hong Kong and asked if I can borrow more money." Despite having already loaned their son upward of $200,000 to get his business off the ground, his parents agreed to help him out once again. "My family believed in me," Lee says. "They had seen the success I'd had up until that point in other restaurants, so they agreed to let me borrow the money in order to move ahead on the project."

With the money secured, the deal was able to proceed. In Lee's eyes, all was well between the three partners. But trouble was brewing. "A month later they called a meeting," he recalls. "Scott says they're going to scrape the restaurant and the brewpub, and he's going to do the comedy club by himself." Despite having just invested another $150,000 of his family's money into what Lee believed was a partnership, Hansen and Janucz also suggested that he should work for free at the Minneapolis Comedy Gallery location in order to pay down the trio's debt, since it was Lee's idea to open a new location. Lee was blindsided. The numbers game wasn't on his side.

"I said, 'You just asked me to borrow money from my family, and now you're going to scrape my side to make yours more profitable? That doesn't work,'" Lee recalls. "So Scott and Rick said, 'Let's do a vote.' And the two of them outvoted me. So I said that I'd walk away, but that they had better keep paying the loan to the bank and not mess with my family's money. Sure enough, thirty days later, Scott and Rick quit paying the guaranteed loan, and the banker takes the money. Now they have the business, and I owe all of this money. They told me, 'If you try and mess with us or sue us, we'll put the company into Chapter 11.' And that's how I lost $350,000."

Scott Hansen passed away in late 2021. But his version of the story couldn't have been more different. "The reason I opened the St. Paul club without Louis was that he was rejected by the St. Paul Port Authority," Hansen shared in an email. "The reason given to me by Gordon Awsumb, the leasing agent from Galtier Plaza, was large transfers of money into his account from his family. These made them suspect ties to organized crime. Deposits were in six figures." While the implication that Lee or his family had any connections to organized crime was shocking to begin with, Hansen didn't stop there.

> Here is how Louis tricked all of us. All partners made an initial investment of $100,000. We also added several minor partners that Louis had promised payments to. Rick Janucz made a cash payment secured by his business, I did the same. But Louis, who was a bartender at a bar owned by Janucz, got the same amount from his mother in Hong Kong. He then deposited the $100,000 in a bank and used that as security.
>
> Louis was the treasurer of our corporation. When he got in the accident, he had head injuries and we were told that he would be hospitalized for a long stretch. The next day the partners voted and made Michelle [Hansen's wife] treasurer because she was the treasurer of my comedy business and had been working with the brewpub and bar corporation assimilation. She opened the books and found out Louis had not paid rent, sales tax, or employee withholding for two quarters. She also found a monthly payment to a bank in Forest Lake being made each month. She called the bank and was told that it was for a loan repayment on a $100,000 loan.
>
> The corporation was repaying his initial investment without the knowledge or consent of any of the other partners or shareholders. We met with the bankers, told them that we were no longer going to make the payments on the loan. We couldn't afford it. It was made personally by Louis and he had no authorization to do so through our corporation. One of the bankers then asked "what about the car?" Louis had also used the $100,000 as collateral to buy a new car.
>
> When he returned, he acknowledged that the pay-

> ments were not only wrong but possibly fraudulent and illegal. He was fired immediately. He did not quit.
>
> I renegotiated the lease with Riverplace and they forgave all $100,000 in owed rent, as long as Louis was fired. That had to be in our new lease. I negotiated a payment plan with the state of Minnesota to pay all of our sales tax over $40,000.00
>
> Michelle and I sold our lake cabin and five acres of land that we had just built at a loss, to make a partial payment on the federal withholding tax. That was $60,000. I then negotiated a payment plan for the remaining $70,000.
>
> We found that Louis and his financial advisor, Joe Block, were selling shares of the brewery in $5,000 increments. There were 11 listed investors for a total of $750,000. This had been done to finance the buildout of the bar and brewpub which I had no part of at the time.
>
> I satisfied some of the investors and became part of a lawsuit against Louis for $750,000.
>
> Louis did not show up in court. We won by default and each and all of us were awarded, jointly and severally $750,000.

Lee's reaction to Hansen's detailed and shocking claims is blunt. "In order to have a license to open a brewpub in the eighties, all license holders—including myself—had to go through a BATF [Bureau of Alcohol, Tobacco, and Firearms] background check," Lee shared in the book *Funny Thing about Minnesota.* "It was a long process because I am from Hong Kong. They also had all of my family background as well. And after that, I was granted a brewery license. I think Hansen's statement regarding Chinese immigrants in the US pretty much sums up his character and worldview." Lee's friend Jim Meyer, an employee of Hansen's at the time of the rift, has another, much simpler theory on what happened. "I never liked Rick Janucz. Never trusted the guy," Meyer recalls. "I think he fueled more of it [the disagreement] between them. There just wasn't enough money to split between three people, so Louis got screwed."

Lee spent the next several years scraping to repay his family, with little success. He tended bar around town, and at one point managed a local Olive Garden to make up his seemingly insurmountable debt. Sadly, the work Lee had done to carve his own path in America in the restaurant and hospitality industry had fallen apart and nearly killed him in the process. "I owed my family so much money," he says. "For me it was either, I could try and pay it back, or I could kill myself. So what can I do to repay the debt?"

• CHAPTER 3 •

OPEN FOR BUSINESS

If it were up to Louis Lee, Acme Comedy Company never would have existed. After the fallout with Scott Hansen and the Comedy Gallery, Lee was ready to get as far away from comedy as possible. "When I tell you that I lost everything, I mean *everything,*" Lee says. "So my friend Jim Meyer said, 'To hell with this. You and I can just find a neighborhood bar to open.' So we went to a broker and asked him to find a bar for us to buy."

Beginning with their time together at Trumps, Meyer and Lee often found their way back to one another working in the Twin Cities bar community. "We hit it off pretty good," Meyer recalls. "He was a waiter and I tended bar. We didn't hang out a lot after work, but we became pretty good friends at work. When he moved over with Hansen, he must have seen something in me because he asked if I wanted to come over and work with him. That's when we started to get a little more tight."

Once the Comedy Gallery was open, Lee and Meyer continued to be friends, though they were on opposite ends of the professional spectrum. "Louis was in the office, more behind the scenes," Meyer continues. "We'd still go out and have a cocktail after work, but he didn't work on the floor as much." After Lee's accident, Meyer carried on at the Comedy Gallery, until he received a call one day, an invitation from Lee to partner on a bar. "He needed to find something to get himself out of debt, because he owed his parents quite a bit of money," Meyer says. "He knew he couldn't open it by himself. I mean, I had no money to put into it. My piece was all sweat equity. I could just do what I knew how to do and that was tend bar and that sort of thing. I think he was looking to bring someone in with him just so he wasn't going it alone."

While Lee was in a dire situation, faced with his crippling debt and shaken confidence after the accident and subsequent issues with Hansen, Meyer had a much more free-spirited approach to the new business. "I was bouncing around to different jobs at that point. We were both barely thirty. I had no worries. I was like, *What's the worst that happens? We open a restaurant and it falls on its face? I'll just go down the block and start tending bar again.*" Meyer's laid-back attitude and strong work ethic made him an ideal partner for Lee, and soon the duo began scouting potential locations. But of all the places they could have picked, fate seemed to pull them back toward the very thing Lee was trying to flee, a space with its own complicated comedy past.

For years, Scott Hansen had been leading the charge to establish Twin Cities stand-up comedy venues. But he wasn't the only one. In October 1985, David Wood's Rib Tickler opened in the Itasca Building of the warehouse district of Minneapolis. The 250-seat space was billed as an upscale comedy club, with low ceilings, a compact showroom, and an attached dining room. David Wood, a comic from Rochester, worked with an architect to design the space, arranging it so that performers could appear from behind a curtain and face the entire audience head-on, as opposed to seating people in a semicircle, where some could only glimpse the comics' side profiles while they performed.

The club was somewhat ahead of its time for Minneapolis. It enforced a strict no-smoking policy and established a reputation as a place for clean comedy material. Over the years, the club managed to attract national talent like Dana Carvey and Kevin Nealon, along with live magic acts that became one of its specialties. By 1990, though, Wood decided to leave the club amid rumors of infighting among members of the ownership group, as well as a desire to focus on his own comedy career full time.

After Wood exited, the club limped along for a few more months, changing management several times. "The people who owned the place were like a bunch of stockbrokers, and they treated it like a country club," Lee says of the club's history. "After Wood left, the manager took over, and he was a restaurant man, not a comedy man. He ran it right into the ground." Even Hansen himself managed the space for a brief period, trying out a women's-only club concept that featured all female talent and staff. Despite having a well-established brand name in the area when it came to comedy, Hansen was unable to pull the club out of the hole it was in.

Once Hansen left, a local open micer who had inherited quite a bit of money decided to invest in the club and turn things around. He soon learned a hard lesson about managing a comedy club—and about comedians. "He hired this comedian named Pat Paulsen," Lee recalls. "He was a comedian in the eighties who would run for president every four years as a publicity stunt. The comic who was running the room hired Pat and had to give him a big guarantee [money regardless of ticket sales]. The show didn't sell, and the comic lost his shirt. That's when everything really went to hell."

The owners were motivated to get out from under their collapsing investment right around the time Lee and Meyer were searching for their new venture. But Lee didn't see the stars aligning for his return to comedy just yet. "The restaurant they had wasn't doing anything, and they made us an offer to buy half of the place for $40,000," Lee recalls. "I came in and met with them, but I took a look at the balance sheets and told Jim no way. Sure, I could raise $40,000 and help make them whole, but that doesn't solve any of the problems they're having." Lee recommended to Jim that they wait to see what would happen to the space in the coming weeks. Sure enough his prediction rang true, and just two months after their meeting, the Rib Tickler closed its doors for good.

Lee and Meyer were ready to give the enterprise a second look. But they weren't the only ones. Hansen, who was opening new comedy rooms on what seemed like a weekly basis, put in a bid on the space, intending it to be the final piece of his comedy empire in the Twin Cities. However, after meeting with Lee, the City of Minneapolis, which had seized the property, made the surprising decision not to partner with Hansen. "I told them what I knew about how Hansen was running the comedy business," Lee says plainly. "I told them that it wasn't sustainable, and if he ran this space the way he was running his other clubs, they'd be right back in the same position a year from now. So they called me and said, 'OK, Louis, we'll give you a shot.' "

Because the space was large, recently abandoned, and located in a not-so-great spot for casual foot traffic, Lee and Meyer got a deal that never would have happened in a more booming area of Minneapolis. "The city gave us a deal you couldn't pass up," Meyer recalls. "I can't remember if they financed it or just gave really good terms, but we got all of the equipment in the restaurant for pennies on the dollar. You never would have been able to open a restaurant that size and make it work if it were brand new. They always say the third owner of a place is the one who makes the money." Lee and Meyer would be the third owners of the space, though they intended to use only the bar and restaurant. "I wanted no part of a comedy club," Lee says matter-of-factly. "I absolutely refused. Jim and I just wanted the restaurant and the bar."

As they began building out their new space, the partners recognized that having a custom-built showroom sitting va-

Jim Meyer and Louis Lee prepare for the opening of Acme Comedy Company. *Courtesy Jen Bryce*

cant didn't make business sense, and they were eventually persuaded to soften their stance on reentering the comedy world. "We had this room, and we didn't really know what else to do with it," says Meyer. "Our only other option would have been to empty it out and turn it into a dining room, but we knew we needed some sort of a hook to get diners in the place. That particular space needed some type of entertainment. It was off the beaten path, and there is no way we could have done anywhere near the restaurant business that we did if it hadn't been for the club."

Lee reluctantly went along with the plan. "A friend convinced me to give comedy another shot," Lee says. "I agreed, but all along my plan was that once the comedy scene gets on its feet, someone else can have that part and I just want the restaurant." At the time, the comedy bubble had begun to burst. Stand-up comedy had saturated the market, both locally and nationally. More and more clubs. More restaurants and venues. And an endless string of shows and a lack of talent to fill the lineups. Worse: the stand-up secret was out. It wasn't just club owners and restaurant managers who knew that stand-up comedy was a low-cost, high-return way to draw customers. Television networks were starting to get in on the act. A new basic cable channel called Comedy Central launched in the spring of 1991, providing a nonstop stream of stand-up to the masses in the comfort of their own homes.

The influx of comedy and the competition with Hansen made it nearly impossible for the new club to find talent. "A lot of people were afraid to come to work [at Acme] because they thought, what if we go work over there, [and] these guys don't make it?" says Meyer. "What if they shut down in six months—which we probably should have—and then I have to try and go back?" To help get the comedy side up and running, Lee and Meyer partnered with a comic named Kristin Andersen and put her in charge of booking. Andersen was a fast-rising comic who had made a big splash locally in the late eighties working in Scott Hansen's circuit of clubs. She moved to Los Angeles for a few years to make a bid toward the next step in her entertainment career, before heading back to Minnesota right around the time Lee and Meyer were looking to launch Acme.

"Kristin approached us," says Meyer. "We didn't know what we were doing and who we should talk to. She liked us from the Comedy Gallery days, and I think she had a falling out with Scott, which is why she wanted to do some things with us too." A comic who was well connected locally, with strong ties out west due to her time in LA: Andersen was the perfect choice to help grow the new club. "I told her that we'd do the same thing as usual," Lee recalls. "You keep the money from the door; I keep the money from food and drinks."

With the pieces mostly in place, Acme Comedy Company

Comedian Kristin Andersen, who was the first booker in Acme Comedy Company history. *Courtesy Jen Bryce*

opened for business on November 8, 1991. That night, Mr. Elk and Mr. Seal, an a capella comedy duo who were protégés of Twin Cities comedy breakout star Joel Hodgson, headlined the show, along with fast-rising up-and-comer Frank Conniff. Over the next few weeks, the club featured a mix of local favorites like Susan Vass, Mary Rowles, and Rob Benton, alongside more unique acts like Puke N Snot (a comedy duo best known for their performances at the yearly Minnesota Renaissance Festival) and a clown called T. C. Hatter. But also gracing the Acme stage was a pocket of comics who had been turned down or cast out by Hansen.

"When I came to Minnesota in the summer of '86 or '87, I was trying to get into the Comedy Gallery," says Jackie Kashian, a Wisconsin transplant who spent years working the local comedy circuit. "I was trying to get in with Scott and his brother Tom, because Tom booked all of the shitty road gigs. I did a little hanging around, did some shows at the weird freak show women's club concept that Scott had for a while, but I didn't really get too far." Despite the fact that Acme was new and unproven, Kashian says she could tell the difference in

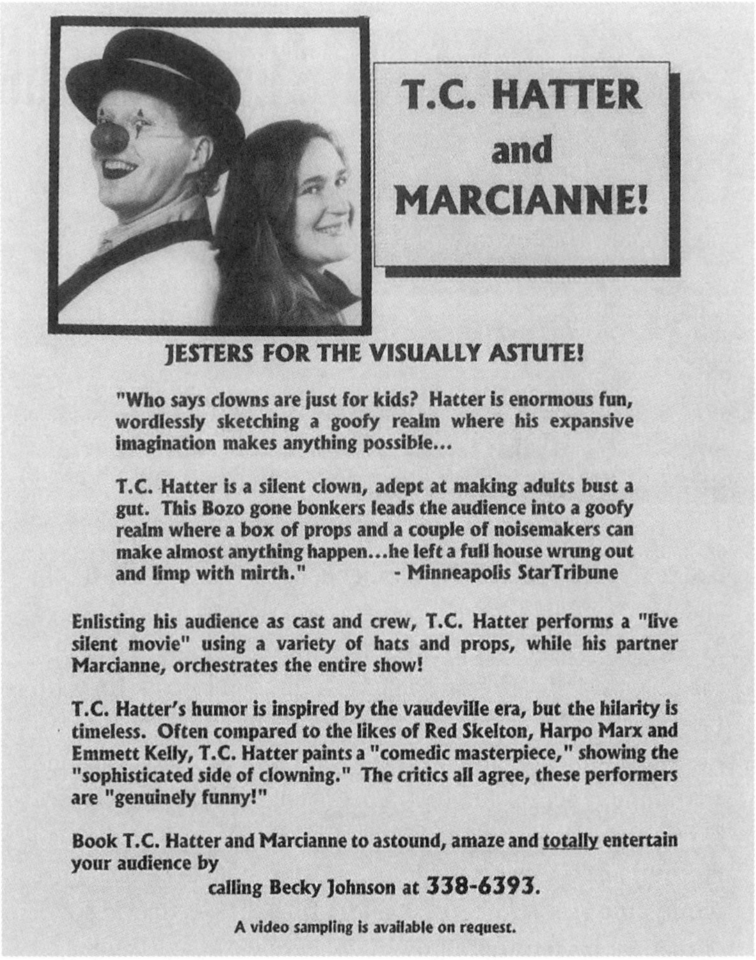
T.C. HATTER
and
MARCIANNE!
JESTERS FOR THE VISUALLY ASTUTE!
"Who says clowns are just for kids? Hatter is enormous fun, wordlessly sketching a goofy realm where his expansive imagination makes anything possible...
T.C. Hatter is a silent clown, adept at making adults bust a gut. This Bozo gone bonkers leads the audience into a goofy realm where a box of props and a couple of noisemakers can make almost anything happen...he left a full house wrung out and limp with mirth." - Minneapolis StarTribune
Enlisting his audience as cast and crew, T.C. Hatter performs a "live silent movie" using a variety of hats and props, while his partner Marcianne, orchestrates the entire show!
T.C. Hatter's humor is inspired by the vaudeville era, but the hilarity is timeless. Often compared to the likes of Red Skelton, Harpo Marx and Emmett Kelly, T.C. Hatter paints a "comedic masterpiece," showing the "sophisticated side of clowning." The critics all agree, these performers are "genuinely funny!"
Book T.C. Hatter and Marcianne to astound, amaze and totally entertain your audience by
calling Becky Johnson at 338-6393.
A video sampling is available on request.

The early days of Acme featured eclectic acts, as the club tried to keep the comedy business afloat during an industry downturn. *Courtesy Jen Bryce*

attitude between it and other clubs right away. "[Acme] was a place of business, and it was treated that way," she explains. "A lot of clubs were, and still are, treated like hobby bars. It's guys who should have bought a liquor store or a strip club, and they bought a comedy club instead. When I started working in Madison, it was at a club owned by Sam Kinison's brother.

Jackie Kashian was one of the very first comedians to view Acme as her home club. *Courtesy Jen Bryce*

There was cocaine, sex workers, violence. They wanted to be rock stars. When you came to Acme, you knew not to mess with the staff or bartenders, you knew that you'd be paid fairly, and you knew nobody who worked there was going to be gross."

While the club was still struggling just to break even, Lee found ways to give back to the community that had supported him early on. The club hosted a weeklong benefit for the Aliveness Project, a community center in Minneapolis focused on serving individuals with HIV. This cause was especially important to Lee because many people he knew from his earlier restaurant days had passed away from the disease years prior. "These were my friends," he recalls. "And a lot of them used [the Aliveness Project], so how could I not help them?"

Despite early momentum, things were already getting shaky. Though Andersen kept the calendar full with a steady stream of comics for the first few months, her relationship with Lee and Meyer quickly began to deteriorate. "After a few months, she said that she didn't have any money to hire enough comics to come work," says Lee. "And a lot of the comics had already been told by Scott that they couldn't work at Acme or they wouldn't be able to work for him. So she said, 'Why don't I try and headline three or four times over the next few months to cut the costs down?' And I looked at her and said, 'No. That's not the way I want to start a comedy club. You have to do something different.' She didn't agree, so I looked at her and said 'you've got to go.' "

Andersen, however, has a much different recollection of the falling out. In a 2021 interview with the Minnesota Historical Society, Andersen pulled no punches in providing her side of the story. "I worked really hard, and had friends that came in and helped me put that club together," she said. "I worked myself to death. I used my connections from Los Angeles, and then within three months they voted me out. I had nothing." Having cut ties with Hansen due to her involvement with Acme, Andersen said she had no other comedy avenues available to her. When asked why Lee might have wanted her out, Andersen said she believes it was far more malicious than a difference of opinion. "He didn't need me anymore," she said. "He didn't want to pay me. He wanted my hard work and my connections, and then wanted the whole thing for himself. He didn't have a reason and he didn't need to have a reason. He had a plan from the beginning."

While Lee and Andersen both seemed to place the blame on differing booking and business philosophies, Meyer remembers things differently. "It fell apart because she wanted more money," he says. "At that point, me and Louis were flipping a coin each week to see who got to cash their check. She was getting greedy on us and threatened to pull out, and we called her bluff." Regardless of whose story is true, the result was the same. Andersen left the club for good. In her place, Lee brought in Becky Johnson.

Johnson was married to a comic named Gary Johnson, who was one of the first "official" stand-up comedians in Minnesota, after winning a comedy contest at a bar called Mickey

Finn's in Northeast Minneapolis back in the late 1970s. Becky had been arranging shows for her husband throughout the Midwest, but was also booking acts at William's Bar during the original comedy boom. However, once Hansen took over William's, Johnson parted ways. That's when Lee came calling. "I was excited about it," Johnson said in an interview with Racket, an online alternative publication in the Twin Cities. "It was a big, beautiful room, for starters. Louis and I talked about the comedians' needs, his budget, and if I thought I could work with it and still present something viable."

Money remained extremely tight for Lee and Meyer, who came up with a unique proposition to help bring on Johnson. "At the time, we were so poor that we could only offer her a few hundred dollars a week," recalls Lee. "But we figured if we could have Gary emcee the shows, we could pay him to do that and now the money for both of them isn't that bad. At least not in 1992." Johnson agreed to come aboard, along with Gary, who became the house emcee for Acme. Now they just needed to get some new talent through the doors. "We needed to find the comedians who didn't work the big clubs, because the established comics weren't allowed to work for Acme," says Lee.

Over the next several months, Johnson did exactly that, using her Rolodex of road comics to bring in newer names to the club. Often, road comics are competent though not necessarily creative comedians who have found a working formula for comedy and are comfortable performing the same show in any town that will have them. While a far cry from the glory days of stand-up comedy in Minnesota, it was enough to continue building an audience. "It was a B room," says J. Elvis Weinstein, a comedy wunderkind who began working in Hansen's clubs at just fifteen years old, befriending Lee and Meyer back when they were bartending in the Comedy Gallery. Johnson booked Weinstein to headline Acme early in her time at the club, a fact Weinstein himself still finds funny. "I wasn't like a good get for them," Weinstein laughs. "But Scott had jammed them up with all of the agents and everything, so you could see they weren't really getting that great of quality acts, myself included. I'd say it was a lot of comics you would see in a Sioux Falls, South Dakota, Holiday Inn bar. I had been in plenty of B rooms at that point in my career, and it felt like that."

While working to find and book decent acts who could fill a sixty-minute headlining slot, Johnson also expanded the club's reach thanks to her ties to the Seattle comedy scene, which allowed her to bring in performers like Tim Slagle and Kermet Apio. But during Johnson's time with the club, some of Scott Hansen's most loyal comedian friends began to defy the understood policy and take the stage at Acme. "Alex Jackson was the first one," Lee remembers. "Then it was C. Willi Myles, and then Bill Bauer, and then Alex Cole. And as Scott's business deteriorated, the floodgates started to open." "Scott was a classic bully," says Weinstein. "If you pushed back on him, he'd usually fold. He was always very good to me, but whenever he would kind of pull that kind of stuff, I'd just kind of be like, 'Really, Scott?' and he'd kind of shrug and let it go. I think a lot of people started to figure that out."

Though Acme was bringing in newer talent than Hansen, the comedy kingpin wasn't going to go down without a fight. Hansen would have his employees call Acme and make reservations, then no-show on the night of the event. It got so bad at one point that the club started taking down phone numbers because dozens and dozens of ticket reservations turned out to be bogus. Lee was more than comfortable hitting back. "I'm thinking, 'I'll help Scott out.'" he laughs. "I'm going to throw ten thousand free tickets out every week, so that nobody is paying for comedy. When you make your money on ticket sales, and no one is buying tickets, nothing else works. I was thinking that I can still sell drinks and food to survive."

Survive was the operative word. During the first three years of running Acme, Lee estimates that he lost another $150,000.

But even though his finances were shaky, his family's support for his dream never wavered. "Every summer I went to my family and said that I needed another five, ten, or fifteen grand," Lee recalls. "And amazingly they had enough faith in me to help. They knew I was working seven days a week. It's really just me, Jim, a bar manager, and a kitchen manager. I tended bar, I cooked. The only thing I didn't do was tell jokes. Me and Jim, from 1991 through '93, we had an agreement that one of us would pay our rent late every month until we got an eviction notice."

The business side was proving to be a struggle, but the talent side was booming. Johnson continued to bring in talent, while finding ways to drum up publicity for the fledgling club. "We were booking really fun shows," Johnson said. "We were doing whatever we could do to get the press interested. We wanted to build a good reputation and gain recognition. Not just in Minneapolis, but also with the national comedy community." Margaret Smith, Carl Wilson, and Stephanie Hodge all came in during Johnson's tenure as Acme's booker, demonstrating her ability to find the diamonds in the rough. "At the risk of sounding arrogant, I had a good eye for funny," she said. "I listened to the material and not the audience reaction. I was looking for comics who were polished, professional, clever, and clean." Another key difference maker, she says, was having Gary as the emcee. "Comics really liked working with my husband," she said. "He had a really relaxed style and had a knack for getting the audience focused and relaxed and ready to laugh."

By 1993, major changes began to take place in the club. The audience was slowly growing, and the business was staying afloat, but life began to pull Meyer and Johnson in different directions. For Johnson, the insane hours she had to put in at the club had begun to wear on her, especially as she was also taking care of her young family. Eventually, she decided to leave the club in favor of a more regular schedule with a law firm. Her legacy, though, endured. "I would say the paying audience increased by 30 percent by the end of the first year," she shared proudly. Lee echoes her sentiments. He credits Johnson with helping to set the tone for the kind of club Acme would become. "Becky kept the talent coming in that first wave," he says. "She helped me to really understand what was missing in comedy, and to see the difference between the real comics and the road comics."

Meanwhile, Meyer says the long hours he and Lee were spending together, combined with some personal issues he was managing at home, made his decision to exit the club something of a no-brainer. "Louis and I were getting to that point where things were a little tense," he remembers. "If it came up to a vote on anything, I would lose because he had his whole family backing him. And I get that, because they had a huge nut in there that they needed to protect. It just seemed like the right time. My father was dying, and I was spending more time over there taking care of him, and it got to the point where I was like, *Do I want to stay down here and potentially lose a friend over a business?* And the answer was absolutely not."

Meyer informed Lee of his decision to leave the business, and Lee agreed to do right by his partner. "He came to me and said that he can't do it anymore," Lee recalls. "I told him that I didn't blame him at all. I said, 'I can't pay you a big chunk of money, but I can get you X amount of dollars every week over the next few months.'" But as Meyer walked away from Acme, his friendship with Lee was still intact. "He probably sensed it was coming," Meyer says of his decision to leave. "You start to know when someone isn't happy. Would it ever have come down to him pushing me out? I don't know. From a business standpoint I could probably see it, but who knows? We left on great terms, and I'd even still go back and help tend the bar at Christmastime when he needed the help."

Acme was on a steady incline, inching slowly toward the goals Lee had set out for himself years earlier. "I told myself that this club was something I believed in, and I needed to stick with it and see if I was right," Lee says. It was time for Lee to take the club to the next level—in terms of the talent, the audience, and the way he conducted business. Hansen's comedy empire had become a shell of its former self, ceding ground and leaving Lee with the opportunity to expand his business without worrying about his rival working against him. But reaching that next level wasn't going to be as easy as simply booking new acts or changing up his marketing tactics; he needed to change the culture of stand-up comedy in Minnesota, a culture that had been cultivated over the course of decades but was now outdated. He needed to correct the mistakes of the past if he wanted to open doors to the future.

That's when he decided to take a trip to the Mall of America.

· CHAPTER 4 ·

TEAR IT DOWN, BUILD IT UP

Today, Acme is revered not just for the quality of its comedy but for the quality of the audience. Its patrons are courteous, thoughtful, and willing to let performers stretch themselves creatively. But that wasn't always the case.

"One of my favorite stories was when I headlined the club early on, and I had my mom, my grandma, my wife, and my stepson in the audience," says J. Elvis Weinstein. "And there was a biker gang at this particular show. So I started getting into it with them, and my mom was fucking terrified. In the end, I won. I remember I said to one of them, 'What's your name?' and he goes, 'Lightbulb.' And I said, 'I'm guessing it's not because you had a good idea.' At that point they started buying me drinks and everything was good, but it definitely wasn't the audience it is now." While Weinstein was able to weather the storm that night, Lee knew that in order for Acme to grow into something new, different, and sustainable, he needed to do more than just create a new ecosystem of comedians: he need to craft a new kind of crowd for this new brand of comedy.

Hansen's comedy empire, despite its fall from former glory, was still synonymous with stand-up comedy in Minnesota. His audiences retained a nostalgia for the good old comedy days that peaked in the eighties, but the new generation of potential fans saw local stand-up as an outdated relic of a once-popular art form. To combat that stigma, Lee decided to reach a crowd with no real knowledge or memory of that earlier era. "I decided that I'm going to move the flag backwards," Lee explains. "I'm going to make my club eighteen and up. I'll get the college kids in. I know they don't drink, but they haven't seen the good comedy that we had in the early eighties, just the shitty stuff. So I'm going to lower the age, I'm going to make the open mic free, and I'm going to get rid of the two drink minimum like a lot of clubs had. If everything goes right, four years from now those kids that are coming in here at eighteen will be twenty-two, they'll have their first jobs out of college, and they'll have more disposable income."

The strategy was certainly bold, and not conducive to keeping the lights on at a business that was desperately trying to stay afloat from week to week. But Lee saw the long-term opportunity and was prepared to buckle in for the duration. "A lot of clubs were, and truthfully still are, more concerned about selling chicken wings than comedy," says Weinstein. "But he didn't care. He wanted it to be a place where comedy came first." Jackie Kashian echoes Weinstein's feelings on the unusually patient strategy: "What's amazing is he created a club that catered to all ages, hired a waitress or two to serve them waters, and trained them so that they would come back much later on to eat, drink, and be merry. But in the meantime, he was educating them as comedy fans."

Even as he was pursuing his ambitious strategy for building the new Acme audience, Lee needed to figure out how to build back the talent pool. He needed to give this new audience something worth watching. To do that, he needed someone to take over booking duties from Becky Johnson. Jennifer Bryce (known as Jennifer Lack in her Acme days) had previously worked for Hansen as the marketing director for his Comedy Gallery locations. She and Lee had crossed paths during their shared time at the club, but after Hansen let her go, Bryce had

Jen Bryce brought her marketing expertise and love of comedy to the club at a pivotal point in Acme's history. *Courtesy Jen Bryce*

no interest in ever going back to comedy. "Comedy just died," Bryce recalls of the nineties. "Every bus driver bought a bar and started a weekend comedy show. I think [local journalist] David Brauer actually wrote a piece when Acme first opened, and the tone was basically, 'Well, comedy is dead and some idiot is still going to open a club. So if you're interested, you better go see a show while you can because it's probably not going to last very long.'"

But after Johnson's exit from Acme, Lee reached out to Bryce and asked her to take over booking duties. And having spent a few years away from stand-up, she decided to take on the challenge. "Louis asked me to come on board and be the marketing director, but what he really had in mind was for me to be the talent agent," she explains. Once she started at the club, Bryce recognized that Lee had a passion for stand-up comedy—and an eye for talent, even if he was reluctant to trust his own taste. "I didn't want to do the booking because I thought Louis should do it," she says. "But that's what he wanted. I took over, but we had a lot of conversations about what he did and didn't like from a comedy standpoint." Having seen the stand-up scene at its best, Bryce felt a personal sense of responsibility in helping to grow both the club and the local comedy scene as a whole. "I wanted to do it because comedy was a dead art form," she says bluntly. "It needed to be revived, and the comedy scene in the Twin Cities was worthwhile." Around the time Bryce came to Acme, another player in the comedy world entered the scene.

Rich Miller came from a comedy family. His brother is *Saturday Night Live* alum Dennis Miller, famous for his work onstage and in front of the camera, while his brother Jimmy has had an incredibly successful career as a producer in Hollywood. Rich followed a similar path, managing several thriving comedy clubs around the country, while also working as a talent agent for many comics along the way. Much like anyone else who had followed the comedy path through Minnesota, Miller had worked with Scott Hansen years earlier and helped make his clubs a success.

By 1993, Miller was a part of an ownership group in Texas that operated several comedy clubs. He returned to Minnesota to run a club called Knuckleheads inside the Mall of America. Miller was well connected and well funded, and this new venue had the advantage of being placed in the newly opened entertainment hotbed of Minnesota. Miller knew right away that his club would cater to a different audience than Acme. "At Knuckleheads you needed the bells and whistles," he says. "I needed someone who was going to pull a chicken out of their rear end." But he also needed local talent to help fill out his lineups. Recognizing the potential for collaboration or conflict with one another, Lee reached out to Miller in hopes of avoiding a repeat of the contentious relationship he had with Hansen.

"I met with Rich in 1993 and said, 'Look, what's good for comedy is good for everybody,'" Lee explains. "'Let's share the local comics, let them get stage time at both clubs, and they'll get better, faster. Let's not play any games. If your open mic is on Sunday, we'll be closed on Sundays.' Our open mic is on Monday, so they were closed on Mondays. The whole market had to work together." Miller quickly agreed with Lee, and appreciated his straightforward approach. "I had crossed paths with Louis in the past and thought he was a good cat," Miller says. "So when he called me and said, 'Let's make a game plan,' I was on board right away. I told him I had my ticket sellers and he had his, but the emcees and features should be allowed to work wherever they want. Let's just space them out so that we don't burn out the market."

Soon, people like John Bush, Michael Thorne, K. P. Anderson, and Darlene Westgor were spending time at both clubs, while Acme and Knuckleheads each worked to carve out their own niches for headlining acts. On Miller's side of the street, names like Nick Di Palo and Ron White became Knuckleheads favorites. Lee and Bryce, on the other hand, needed some more help if they were ever going to get beyond the road comics they had been using and move toward the unique voices that would help shape Acme's sensibility and burnish its reputation in the industry.

T. J. Markwalter was a young agent who was eager to cut his teeth in the stand-up comedy world. He had started his career in New York, before moving to a talent management agency called Omnipop in 1991. (He started with Omnipop the day before Acme hosted its very first show.) Markwalter had contact with Kristin Andersen during her brief time at Acme, but didn't start working with the club until around 1993. "It was very early on in both of our careers," Markwalter says. "But I realized really early how different Louis and Acme were from other clubs. A lot of clubs at that point were chasing heat. They just wanted to book whatever was hot and would sell tickets. Louis didn't care about that. He was concerned with the quality of the comedy. Was it original? Was it funny?

Did they have an original voice? It was more about the art for him than the business, and the business followed."

While Markwalter was eager to provide new, fresh headliners for Acme, Bryce played intermediary between him and Lee. "One thing that was frustrating for me was that T. J. would push us to book some of the early *SNL* [*Saturday Night Live*] guys, and Louis wouldn't let me book them," Bryce says. "Even though they were really funny, they didn't have a solid forty-five minutes of material, and Louis didn't want to book anyone who couldn't fill a solid headliner spot." The names Lee did approve of included people like Adam Ferrara and Andy Kindler, even though audiences hadn't quite caught up to their comedy. "I booked Andy Kindler at Acme in August 1994," Markwalter recalls. "He wasn't everyone's cup of tea, but Louis loved him and brought him back. He was a real comic's comic, and I think he even walked the room at the club at one point, but Acme was always supportive."

Others, like a young up-and-comer named Kevin James, were less than ready for Minnesota, or at least its weather. "My weekday mornings would be getting really hungover comedians to radio interviews really early, and then sitting on the floor of the studio and wondering what I was doing with my life," laughs Bryce. "With Kevin James, I was super pregnant and he was in town during a massive snowstorm. So I'm driving him to an interview and we're sliding all over the road, and Kevin is freaking out because he thinks he's going to have to deliver my baby in a snowbank." (He didn't.)

With the pieces finally in place, Acme could start down a path to mature into Lee's vision for what the club—and the local comedy scene as a whole—could be. "While everyone else was collapsing, we were growing," says Lee. "Our open mic went from twenty to thirty people who would show up every Monday, then it became fifty or sixty people. We started getting more people in our comedy contest in the summer. And then we also had the scene in Austin that was really starting to mature too. There was a lot of good talent, and with Rich's connection we were able to hire them and start to arrange so that our comics from Minnesota could go there to work." Bryce says she could see the changes in the audience beginning to happen, albeit slowly. "The size of our crowds would depend on what companies came in," she recalls. "We had a lot of different kinds of audiences. One night you'd have two hundred people from United Healthcare. The next night it would be people who really enjoyed the arts. They liked music and comedy and wanted to see what it was all about. And the audiences were getting smarter. They'd take the ride with the comics. We had everyone from church groups to biker clubs showing up. It was really fun to watch."

By 1995, things had begun to turn around. Lee no longer needed to borrow money from his family, and the relationship between Acme and Knuckleheads had allowed both clubs to flourish. The Minnesota comedy scene as a whole had started to rekindle some of the magic that had seemed long gone just a few years earlier. "The local comics were getting good so fast because they had so much stage time," Lee says. "The contest was rolling, and I was able to tap into the Seattle and San Francisco scenes. I started to realize what I liked and followed my instincts."

Markwalter also started to recognize the logic of Lee's booking style, and he began to craft his clientele to meet Acme's standards. "By the mid-nineties comics started asking me about coming to Acme," says Markwalter. "By '95, '96 it was a known entity. People looked at Denver, Los Angeles, and Acme in the same vein. Sometimes I would get a client who really wanted to get in there, but I knew it wasn't Louis's style. I'd still have the responsibility to my client to ask, but I knew what he did and didn't want. One time I had an act, Ángel Salazar, who was one of my bigger acts. He was in a bunch of films with Al Pacino; he would always sell tickets, and crowds would go nuts for him. I wouldn't pitch him in a million years to Louis. Not because I didn't think he was funny, but he'd be running around saying, 'Sheck it out' and making jokes like, 'I just got my Green Card' and hold up a hubcap. He could go to any Funny Bone in the USA and just destroy, but I would never pitch that to Louis because I just knew it wasn't his style."

While Markwalter was bringing some talent to the club, other comics were taking matters into their own hands to get stage time at Acme. "Doug Stanhope drove here and he was living in his car," says Bryce. "So I said, 'I'll give you three minutes.' The next night I had him come back up and do like eight minutes. At that point we hired him as a host. He was just brilliant. I think we actually let him live in our comedy condo for a while." But as Stanhope is quick to clarify (and then re-muddy), "I was actually booked at Knuckleheads and drove over to Acme for their open mic . . . I mean, I wasn't, like, living in my car. But I didn't have an actual home. So I guess maybe I was? I don't know." Despite getting his first real taste of stand-up while living in Las Vegas, Stanhope quickly recognized that the Twin Cities scene aligned with where his life was at the time. "I never had a home club," he says. "I started out in Vegas, which no one should ever fucking do. But Acme and my youth coincided perfectly. It was an era of my life, like 1992 to 1995. We got away with so much shit back then. People would go onstage fucked up. It was a recklessness of no one having expectations of you or your act."

Two other Acme mainstays made their way to the club for the first time during the same period; both of them went on to achieve major success. "We had the [US Comedy Arts] Festival come around '95 or '96, and that's where I first met Frank Caliendo," adds Lee. "That was the same time that Nick Swardson really started to pop. He went to Aspen that year and popped way too soon." Swardson was a prime example of what Lee had set out to do with his new comedy philosophy. After coming to the club's open mic at eighteen, Swardson

Frank Caliendo (at right in both photos) arrived at Acme early in his career, and was one of the first club regulars to "pop" in the nineties. *Courtesy Acme Comedy Company*

began frequenting the open mic sets, and eventually the club hired him. Other, more prominent comics, like Alex Jackson, had been staples of the local comedy scene for years and had begun to set the precedent that established comics could work Acme despite having a previous relationship with Scott

Hansen. "I think Alex was one of the first headliners to cross over," Bryce says. "He knew his worth and wasn't going to let anyone tell him where he could or couldn't perform. Once he came over, others started to follow."

Though Lee was becoming more involved in booking and curating talent, he was still keenly aware of the potential for conflict between the booker and the comics. He had seen the issues Hansen dealt with and the consequences those issues can have on the health of a club. "I found out that the booker has a lot of power," Lee laughs. "And you can easily get messed up in your head. You think you're bigger than you actually are." Even though Lee was exerting more influence on the comedy side of Acme, he remained wary. His whole comedy career seemed like a series of cautionary tales and hard-learned lessons that all counseled staying behind the bar. But in 1996, Bryce had a baby and had to bow out of her booker duties, leaving Lee with a choice. "I had someone named Greg Langer who took over for a little bit," Lee recalls. "He had another day job but spent a lot of time hanging around the club. But after a little while I remember thinking, *No, this isn't how you book comedy*. At that point I was like, I have to do this." Despite the convictions he so strongly held when Acme first opened, Lee was no longer on the sidelines. He was officially and personally back in the comedy game.

Late 1996, five years into Acme's existence, was a major turning point, not just for the club but for the whole Twin Cities comedy scene. Scott Hansen closed his final Comedy Gallery location. Citing legal entanglements that arose from the Galtier Plaza club's bankruptcy, competition from casinos to hire talent, and stress on him and his family, Hansen told the *Star Tribune* that his last remaining location had seen profits dip from $25,000 a week at its peak to just $5,000 a week. "It's hard to keep up with the bills," Hansen said in the article. "Making a clean break from the club is like taking an albatross from around my neck." Even as Hansen's clubs struggled

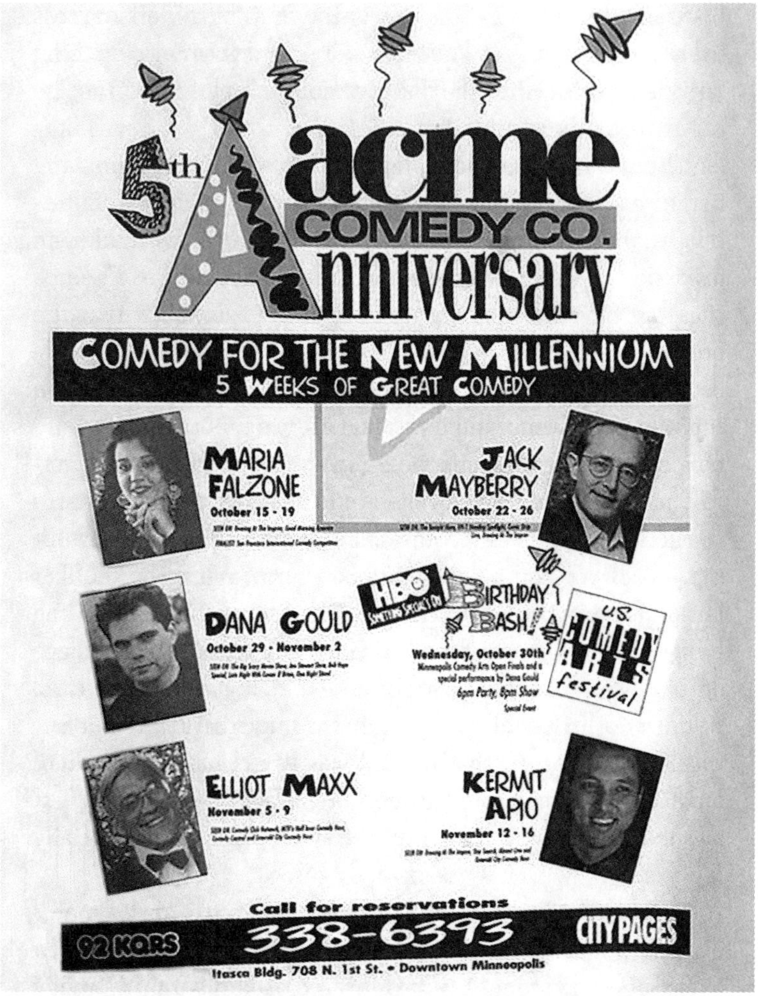

An advertisement for Acme's small but mighty fifth birthday party back in 1996. *Courtesy Jen Bryce*

and consistently declined into the mid-nineties, Acme and Knuckleheads continued to thrive. "I don't think comedy is a sad story at this point," Lee said in the same article. "It's like the early eighties again. People are struggling, but that's when they crank out a great product."

With the Comedy Gallery's closure, the talent floodgates were open. Lee's relationships with Miller and Markwalter put him in prime position to identify and book acts that would fit the tastes and tenor of his audience without the same challenges he'd had during Acme's early years. "Without T. J. and Rich there would be no Minneapolis comedy scene," Lee says. "Having those connections was the reason we were able to keep new talent coming to town during those first few years." Plenty of that talent was on display during the club's five-year anniversary celebration that fall, which featured acts like Dana Gould, Jack Mayberry, and Maria Falzone.

Lee had begun to find his groove and to see the fruits of his labors, while setting the pieces in place for an even brighter, more ambitious future. "I never knew why he went with the name Acme," Miller laughs. "He told me it was to be first in the phone book. I never cared for the name. But aside from that, Louis proved that he had the business mind to stick around when Scott couldn't." The baton had been passed. Twin Cities comedy was no longer just the slow end of an earlier golden age. It was now the rapid birth of a new one. And Lee was at its center. "Louis will always be a priority to me no matter how far I go or how big I get," says Markwalter. "I would never delegate him to anyone else. It's too special of a relationship and took too long to get to this level. He's stuck with me."

Lee had proven that his theory of comedy and his philosophy of running a comedy club were correct. It was time for Lee to finally take the wheel and create some stars of his own.

· CHAPTER 5 ·

THE NEW CLASS

Even after Hansen's empire had fallen, Lee continued to hire new managers to help run Acme. But he had finally embraced the role of comedy kingpin. Beyond booking the acts and marketing them to a new audience (an audience he conceived of and created), Lee had started to look at the talent inside the club. Lee's booking philosophy went beyond importing exciting acts from larger markets. He wanted to do more than just keep his audience entertained and his business running. Lee was interested in helping the craft of comedy itself; he wanted to develop new comedians and set them up for success beyond Acme.

"I used to watch the open mic every week," Lee recalls. "I'd sit in the back and take notes on all of the comics." By that point, Acme's weekly open mic would get upward of twenty to thirty hopefuls, and Lee would watch them carefully, paying close attention to their stage presence, creativity, and confidence. From among these hopefuls emerged a new generation of local comedians who went on to enjoy success far beyond the local scene.

Nick Swardson

By Lee's admission, the first few years of Acme were all about rebuilding both the talent pool and the audience. The emphasis was on pulling in young people.

After a teenage start to his career at Acme, Nick Swardson went on to become arguably the most famous, successful comedian in the club's history. *Courtesy Acme Comedy Company*

Part of Acme's investment in youth was purely economic. It adopted a long-term financial strategy of attracting new customers who would fall in love with Acme as college students and then spend money at the club once they graduated and landed their first jobs. But Lee also wanted to show that a booker who was paying attention could still find and develop decent local stand-up acts following the bubble-burst period of the early nineties. During the first five years of the club, he began to draw an audience and showcase diamonds in the rough from around the country. But locally, comedy still wasn't seen as "cool." On February 12, 1996, that all changed.

Nick Swardson was a nineteen-year-old kid from St. Paul who had an improv past and not a lot of prospects for his future. "My family had no money. Single mother, my grades sucked in high school, college definitely wasn't an option," Swardson recalls. "I had started acting and doing improv in high school, and I decided I wanted to try stand-up. I actually thought stand-up was kind of corny and contrived because improv was so intense. Plus I only really knew about stand-up from the eighties, where everyone was wearing piano ties and shit like that." Swardson wasn't the only person in his social circle who had reservations about stand-up, either. "People would tell me, like, 'Stand-up is dead. It's over.' The eighties were so big and the boom period was so big that when that stopped, it was over," he recalls. "Clubs were folding all over the country, and people told me, like, 'It's done.' But I still really wanted to try it."

Despite having never set foot in the club before, Swardson performed his first-ever stand-up set at Acme's open mic—and blew away the audience as well as the management. "I just fucking walked in cold, and it went amazing," he laughs. "It was kind of a blur for three minutes. Then after, Greg Langer, who was the booker at the time, came up to me and said, 'Who are you? What was that? You're wonderful.' I just told him I was an improv guy who wanted to try stand-up, and he told me I should keep coming back. So I did. It's funny because I remember sitting at the bar that night before the show, and I had this diary. And I was a busboy at Planet Hollywood at the time. So I wrote in my diary, 'I'm going to do stand-up for the first time ever tonight at Acme. Someday, I'm going to be on the wall at Planet Hollywood.'" Though his T-shirt wasn't hanging from the wall of a theme restaurant right away (in fact, today his handprints are immortalized in cement at the Planet Hollywood location in Times Square), Swardson became a local comedy sensation almost overnight. "Knuckleheads was actually the first club to pay me," he recalls. "Then Acme hired me right after that. Pretty soon they were having me feature and co-headline."

Six months after Swardson's first time onstage, Acme played host to auditions for the Aspen Comedy Festival, which at the time was the most prestigious and coveted comedy festival in the United States. Each year, major industry players would converge on Aspen for the HBO-sponsored gathering, participating in showcases and networking events, searching for the next superstar primed for movies and sitcoms. The competition aspect included a panel of judges from HBO, as well as event organizers who had seen some of the best in comedy year after year. For Acme to be hand selected to host the auditions spoke volumes of the respect the organizers had for the club, as well as the level of talent that regularly featured on the Acme stage.

Swardson was one of dozens of comics invited to participate in the tryout. He eventually made it to the top ten, earning the chance to perform for a full audience. "I remember Dana Gould was headlining that night," Swardson recalls. "And I thought my set went great. Then I got offstage and Dana said, 'Dude, I bet you just won.' I couldn't believe it. Then he said it again. Like, 'Yeah man, you definitely just won.' After that I went to Aspen and it changed everything for me."

While Langer was still doing the majority of the booking for Acme at that point, Lee had become a central figure in the club, and he offered Swardson some words of encouragement before he made his trip out west. "Louis told me to just go out there, don't overthink it, and just do my thing," Swardson recalls. "I felt way more pressure when I got to Aspen because everyone is like, do you want a sitcom? Do you have ideas? Do you want to do this or that? But with Louis, he's a pure stand-up connoisseur. He knows stand-up so well. He's just brilliant. He gets it, and he knows who's good at it and doesn't put pressure back on the comics. That's why he's never filtered anybody at his club. I mean, Doug Stanhope is one of my buddies, and he pissed a lot of people off. Louis didn't care." Being a "comic-first" club owner became Lee's calling card.

The prestige and notoriety of being a part of the Aspen Comedy Festival was a massive boost for Swardson's career, and it also served as a conduit to raise Acme's profile on the national stage. "I got all this local press when I got Aspen," Swardson says. "Like this fucking nineteen-year-old kid from

St. Paul is part of this major festival. It was crazy. But after that, all these young people started coming out. Like young people were coming to shows and trying stand-up, and it was crazy." Suddenly, the open mic at Acme became the place to be on Monday nights. Swardson had pumped new, younger life into the local comedy scene, and Acme had all of the pieces in place to channel that momentum into long-term, sustainable success. "It was the best club in the country, and it still is," he says.

Eventually, as his popularity grew, Swardson decided to leave Minnesota and head to New York to chase his dreams and attempt to reach the next level of his career. Before he left, however, the Acme faithful showed just how much they supported him as one of their own. "During one of the open mics, I announced I was moving to New York to try and cut my teeth," Swardson says. "And Dave Mordal passed around a hat to all of the comics that night, and collected money for me. I had no money at the time, and they came together to give me some cash. Even thinking of it now makes me kind of cry. It was very sweet, and it was the kind of environment that Acme had created for us comics."

Though the move out of Minnesota would have its ups and downs ("Acme spoiled me because the crowds were so good. When I went to New York, I actually got booed a couple of times. That's when I realized how amazing the crowds at Acme really are."), Swardson ascended the comedy ranks over the next few years, making the jump from clubs to theaters, while becoming a TV and film superstar. No matter how big he got, however, Swardson always looked to Acme as his home. "I come back every time I'm home because it's the best club in the country," he says. "When I started doing theaters, Louis would promote those shows for me. I just love him so much. He means the world to me. Whenever I'm back I'll post pictures with him and say he's my real dad."

Even decades after Swardson was a fixture of Acme's famed

Anytime Nick Swardson comes home to Minnesota, he takes the time to visit Louis Lee and his home club of Acme. *Courtesy Acme Comedy Company*

open mic night, it's not unusual for him to make the occasional drop-in at the club. "It's so fun to come home," he says. "And Acme is my home. It's great because they'll let me jump in the middle of the show, or come out at the end of the show, whatever. I know it's always going to be a great crowd that gets me. It's like performing in your living room talking to your friends. I'll always come back there."

Pete Lee

Pete Lee was a college student at the University of Minnesota when he first learned about Acme from a *Star Tribune* article written by longtime comedy beat writer Neal Justin and specifically focusing on the club's open mic. "I saw this article that said, come down to Acme for this thing called 'Caught in the Act' [the marketing tagline for Acme's open mic]," Lee recalls. "I had been writing jokes in kind of a minor way before that, but I was way too terrified to get onstage. My roommates kept saying, like, 'You have to try stand-up. You have this incredible gift for making people laugh.' So finally we saw a story that said the next 'Caught in the Act' was going to be a big deal, because it's Nick Swardson's last night in Minnesota."

By that time, Swardson was revered locally. Others saw him as the first and most successful of Acme's farm system of comics. His curtain call from Acme's open mic all but guaranteed a packed house. The event was set for Martin Luther King Jr. Day in 1998. While Lee, who had never been to the club before that evening, was looking forward to the show, he had no idea that he himself would be onstage. "We get down there, and it's packed," Lee continues. "And I find out that my roommates signed me up. I have like an hour to get ready, and I'm scared to death. I was up third on the show that night, and I crushed. Afterward, Louis Lee came up to me and said, 'That was really great. You've clearly been doing this for a while. Anytime you want to come back, you can have a spot on Monday nights.' I was really flattered by that, but I had to tell him, 'Thank you, but this was actually my very first time.' He kind of rolled his eyes like he thought I was lying, but then I came back a few weeks later and bombed my face off and Louis was like, 'OK, that really was your first time.'"

Louis wasn't the only one impressed that first night. Despite being the man of the hour, Swardson himself tracked Lee down after the show. "Nick came up to me and said, 'You're really good. When I come back here in April I'd like you to open for me,'" Lee says. "I'm thinking that this is crazy because that's only like four months away, and this is the first time I've ever done this. But I got his number and he got mine, and I was thinking, like, there's no way he's going to remember this. Then

A young Pete Lee gets onstage at Acme for the very first time. *Courtesy Pete Lee*

the week came when he was back at Acme, and the first night I get this message on my answering machine, and it's like, 'Pete this is Nick. You're supposed to be down here opening for me. You're blowing this.'" Lee was a frequent open mic performer at that point, but the idea of opening for one of the hottest comedians in the country sounded more like a guy trying to be nice than a real business opportunity. Nonetheless, Lee was sure to get himself to Acme that next night. "After I opened for him, Nick goes to me, 'When I asked you to open for me, I meant it.' So I opened for him the rest of the week."

Though this comedy origin story sounds like something straight out of a movie, Lee is quick to point out that his entry into Acme's comedy vortex wasn't all smooth sailing. "The first eight times I went up I had all new material every time," he laughs. "I thought you couldn't repeat anything. After like the seventh time that I bombed, Louis took me in the back room and told me, 'You know, you can repeat material.' Which was a huge relief for me."

While Lee had already served as an official opener for Swardson, he declined payment for his performance. He wanted to remain eligible for Acme's Funniest Person Contest later that summer. (In order to maintain the integrity of the "amateur" element of the contest, the rules state that anyone can enter as long as they have never been paid to perform comedy.) While Lee didn't win the competition, he continued to impress Louis enough to be invited to perform at the club during Christmas week. "Back then, instead of having an out-of-town headliner, Louis would have a bunch of local comics perform throughout the week," Lee recalls. "That Christmas week was my first official introduction to professional comedy."

That March, the club hired Lee officially as an emcee, and matched him up with a massive star on the rise, Lewis Black, for his opening week. "Louis said to Lewis, 'This kid has promise. Could you take him to dinner and talk with him a little bit?' And he said that I could come along with him that night for dinner with his friend Lizz," Lee recalls. "I didn't realize he meant Lizz Winstead. That dinner felt like a comedy master class. Lizz even came to the show later that night and said some nice things about my early work. That felt really good."

Connecting the young upstart with two legends of comedy during his very first week *officially* on the job may seem like an incredible, once-in-a-lifetime gift for a new comic. But Louis believed that giving Lee the opportunity to learn from an established, intelligent performer like Black would hopefully steer him away from potential pitfalls that Louis had seen other comics fall into. "Louis was afraid I was going to do some of those old standards and hacky bits," Lee recalls. "He would talk to me about it a lot. He said, 'You want to kill on the road so that you can get booked again, but you don't want to fall into those trappings.' He encouraged me to write things that were true to myself but that also did well in those rooms. That was really important because it taught me how to get along in bigger, more established clubs, and still be able to handle the crowd at a small bar in Wisconsin."

In addition to helping Lee get regular stage time at Acme as well as Knuckleheads across town, Louis found other ways to keep Pete financially afloat while he pursued his dreams. "I had a degree in advertising, and I was working a day job for an ad agency," Lee says. "And at one point I realized that I was making more money taking weekend gigs than I was in my advertising job." Still apprehensive that Lee would put money before art, Louis found ways to keep him connected to the club and focused on developing his comedy the right way. "Louis would give me a lot of emcee weeks, plus a few feature weeks. But he helped me out in a lot of ways financially," Lee continues. "I remember he would hire me to make ads for the back of the menu at the restaurant," Lee laughs. "I would make the ad, write the copy for it. It was an ad for Acme that would only be seen by people eating dinner in the restaurant next door. It was a bullshit job, but Louis gave it to me because he wanted to give me some money but didn't want to just give it to me. That's how much he cared about me not going on the road and sounding like a road comic."

Even after Lee hit the road as a full-time comic, he returned to Acme regularly for the business and creative benefits, but also because of his relationship with Louis. "I consider him to be like a second father to me," Lee beams. "Having him support my career and tell me that he's proud meant everything. And it still does."

Chad Daniels

While Pete Lee was finding his footing at the club, another U of M student named Chad Daniels had started poking around Acme and playing with the idea of getting onstage himself. "I had tried to do some comedy on my own before I went down to Acme for the first time," says Daniels. "But the first time I officially did stand-up in my opinion was May 4, 1998. That was the first time I did Acme's open mic."

That summer, Daniels took part in the annual Funniest Person Contest. While he didn't advance in the competition, he and his friends had the chance to see another Minnesota comedy legend perform that same evening. "Mitch Hedberg was the headliner that night, and I just remember me and my friends were sitting at Denny's on campus the next morning quoting all of his bits," he recalls. "It was just the best."

Despite an unremarkable performance in the Acme contest, Daniels was hooked. He ended up doing an open mic in his hometown of Fergus Falls, Minnesota, later that same summer, where he received the push he needed to get serious about being funny. "That show I was opening for Bill Bauer and Greg Fideler," Daniels recalls. "I did three minutes, and probably two of those minutes were Dennis Miller material that I stole. Bill was super nice to me. He came up afterwards and goes, 'Hey, just so you know, I recognized some of that material as Dennis Miller. But that minute you did of your stuff was really funny. You should try and do more of that.'" Bauer was one of the original Twin Cities comedians who had been part of the Mickey Finn's era in the late 1970s. By the late nineties, he had become an Acme regular, and getting his blessing was a major boost for a young comic like Daniels. "That was the launching point for me to say that I wanted to give this a crack and try and figure out my own stuff," he says.

The next summer, Daniels once again entered the contest at Acme, making it to the finals before ultimately coming up short. But the experience only convinced him to keep trying. "I took a little break after the contest, but then I went pretty hard after that," he recalls. "Once I got bumped up from three minutes to five minutes during the open mic, I started to feel like I was really making progress."

From the first time Chad Daniels tried stand-up at Acme in the late 1990s, he knew comedy needed to be his full-time passion. *Courtesy Acme Comedy Company*

Between Lee and Daniels (along with other up-and-comers like Isaac Witty and John Evans), Acme had begun shaping its new class of comics. But Daniels saw a different path for himself comedy-wise, a path that ran, oddly enough, through Grand Forks, North Dakota. "There was a club called the Westward Ho," Daniels explains. "And there was kind of this rotation of comics where someone from Minneapolis would go there, emcee for like a year, and then come back and be really good. Then they would sort of choose their successor." Daniels spent most of his time in the Dakotas, seeing how comedy was outside of Acme. "I remember going into other clubs and thinking, *Oh no. I lost my virginity to the greatest club there has ever been, and now I have to put up with these other half-wits,*" he says. "You get spoiled. You really get spoiled, and then you go to these other places and they don't care about stand-up. A lot of times they want you to go up there and tell people where the bathroom is. They don't give a shit about the comedians."

While the gigs may not have felt as prestigious as he'd hoped, Daniels was confident by the time he returned to Acme that the reps he had gotten on the road would make him a shoo-in with Lee. He couldn't have been more wrong. "At that time you'd go to Acme's open mic, and when the list would come out it would have three columns: the name, how much time that person gets, and then a column that was blank," he says. "No one knew why there was a column there, but it turns out it was for Louis to take notes on that comic. I went back a few times, and I saw him writing a lot when I'd be onstage. Then one night we had a little meeting in the atrium after the show, and he told me, 'I think you're funny, but since you're working with all of these road dogs, I can smell the road on your bits. You're not a club act; you're a road act.' But then he pulled out those sheets, and he had written down a bunch of ideas for me on how to get better."

Daniels followed that advice, and after building back a repertoire of material that felt personal and fresh enough for Lee's liking, he got hired as an emcee at Acme. "The first couple of times I emceed I thought to myself, *Holy shit. I can't believe I'm working at Acme*," Daniels recalls. "But then it's like, OK. I'm working at Acme, but there are three slots on this show and I have the shittiest one. So how do I get one of these other two spots?" Much as Louis Lee had done with Pete Lee, he encouraged Daniels to take advantage of his time with some of the headliners he was working with, in order to pick up some of their habits. "You have to watch the other comics' sets as the emcee, so that you know when to get them offstage," Daniels explains. "But I remember early on I went into the green room and saw one of the headliners listening back to their early show, to see if they needed to fix anything for the late show. That's when it really clicked for me. Even today, if you get a week at Acme and you spend the whole time sitting in the bar, drinking and bullshitting the entire time, you're wasting a huge opportunity to get better." Just as Lee had hoped, Daniels was starting to pick up on the *craft* of stand-up, something that only develops through repetition and revision.

Daniels continued working his way up the ladder at Acme, and even began to expand his own small but mighty fan base. "One of my favorite stories from when I was emceeing was one time I was getting my hair cut at Regis in Rosedale Mall," he remembers. "The woman cutting my hair was asking about what I did for a living, and I was pretty proud to be like, 'Oh I'm a comic at Acme. I actually have a show tonight.' She asked if I would put her on the list. I said of course. So I put her and her husband on the list for that night, and later I find out that they got a limo and he bought her flowers. Like this was a big date. I could hear them arguing at the ticket window because the box office person said, 'You missed Chad.' And they got mad and said, 'We couldn't have missed him. He's the headliner!' For the record, I never said that. But I couldn't get an appointment at Regis after that."

While the mall salon level of fame was nice, Daniels aspired to more. His professional relationship with Lee continued to grow as time went on, and despite having worked with and emceed for countless comics at all different levels of success, Daniels looked to Lee as a mentor: "I would always ask Louis for any kind of critique that he had because I just wanted to get better." Then in the early 2000s, life changed for Daniels when he became a father for the first time. Like any new parent in their twenties, he found himself nervous, confused, and overwhelmed about his role. Fortunately, his mentor had a little insight of his own. "Our kids are about the same age," Daniels says. "And I called him one time, just run-down, and asked him, 'How are you doing this? How are you working and cooking three meals a day and everything else?' And he told me, 'I don't cook three meals. I cook meatballs and sauce and then I put them in big containers and heat them up throughout the week.'

After that we started talking more about fatherhood and how to troubleshoot life and that kind of shit. It was so much more than comedy. But it was comedy too. He felt like my comedy dad."

Though their bond was stronger than your average comedy club booker-to-comic relationship, it didn't save Daniels from becoming a victim of one of Lee's infamous pranks. "He gave me my first headlining gig," Daniels remembers. "It was a Tuesday because the main act wasn't coming in until Wednesday. So I went out and I thought I had a pretty good set, and then afterward he comes in the back and says to me, 'Chad Daniel—you no headliner,' and then he shuts the door. My fucking hopes and dreams left my body so fast that night. And then he sits on it for a week before he finally tells me that he was kidding. I was like, you can't do that to me. It was so intense and insane and very, very funny. Years later after I recorded an album at the club, the staff got me a cake that said, 'You No Headliner.' It's so funny to talk about now, but at the time I was searching for nooses and stools."

Once he began headlining the club more regularly, Daniels's career would take off. "After you headline Acme, you have an in everywhere," he says. "You could enter these Comedy Central contests, and if you send them a clip of you headlining at Acme? Holy shit. You were sending them a message that said you need to look at me before you look at some guy headlining a bar show." Lee is still like a father figure to Daniels, even after his career took off. "I had two agencies that came to Acme to see me because they wanted to sign me," Daniels recalls. "And Louis vetted them both very well ahead of time. It was almost like a father meeting his daughter's boyfriend a little bit."

That relationship, Daniels says, is one he doesn't see coming to an end as long as they're both still in the business. "I'll never do something locally that doesn't include Acme," he says. "Even if I come to do a theater show in town or something, I'll either do it in partnership with Acme, or I'll just come down there after and do the late show. It means that much to me."

Maggie Faris

Swardson, Daniels, and Pete Lee were among the vanguard of the new generation of comics to show up at Acme the first time and find that they were already home. Meanwhile, another unique voice was crafting a character that was unlike anything else the club had to offer. But for Maggie Faris, that first Acme experience was much, much different. "I started out in 1999 because my sister was a waitress at Acme and I used to go down and hang out and watch the show," says Faris. "I'd always think, *I could do that.* Then I went up and did the open mic one night, and it was a disaster. I did nothing but gay jokes and talked about being a lesbian and I bombed so hard."

While it would be easy to blame the audience for her less-than-impressive comedy debut, Faris recognized that it wasn't their beliefs or comfort level with her personally that made things go south. "I thought I was terrible and wrote a horrible set," Faris remembers matter-of-factly. "I remember I worked as a waitress with [Acme regular] Colleen Kruse and ran my jokes past her. Then when I bombed I called her crying, like, 'None of my jokes worked!' It's a different ball game onstage between what you think is funny and what works up there."

It took Faris another six months before she mustered the courage to get back onstage, albeit not at Acme. This time, she chose to perform in character, an approach that seemed to work much better for connecting with the audience. "I would do these cliché one-liners," she explains. "It would be like, 'They say the grass is always greener on the other side, which is why I only buy my weed from Mexico.' I definitely wasn't comfortable being myself yet, but I knew I was getting funnier."

Faris soon returned to Acme, where she was able to shake off her less-than-ideal debut and find a place for herself in the booming local comedy scene. "I was there all the time," she says. "I studied comedy a lot, and I wrote and wrote and wrote. I remember Pete Lee and I would sit in the stairwell before open mic and just write jokes. A lot of it was just throwing spaghetti against the wall and seeing what stuck, but I got pretty good, pretty quickly."

Soon the club hired Faris. Her character work was unique and so good that she was promoted to a feature act almost immediately. "They hired me in December 1999, and my very first show they had me co-feature," Faris recalls. "I had such a thick character that I don't think they believed I was personable enough to emcee. So instead they would have me co-feature, and I could do my character and just go." Faris soon found herself accepted into the Acme family, alongside comics like Daniels and Lee, as well as Darlene Westgor, Isaac Witty, Dave Mordal, and others. The one person she didn't connect with right away was Louis Lee.

"There was definitely a code of behavior that you followed if you wanted to work there," she recalls. "Rules like never blow the light, never steal material, and never talk to Louis." She chuckles and amends her statement. "Actually, it was like you don't talk to Louis until you're hired there," she clarifies. "When you get hired, everyone is friendly. We would all sit in that bar together until, well, I can't legally tell you what time it was. But we'd be there until it was daylight. Just drinking beer and chain-smoking and laughing and giggling. And Louis was right there. He was part of it. He became more like a pal than a boss."

But Lee still had high expectations of Faris, much like he did for all of the comics who worked the club. "He liked good joke writers. If you came up with the same stuff every week, you wouldn't get to go back. But you could hone your bits and work on them. I decided early on that I wanted to be a comic that happens to be gay, as opposed to being a gay comic. I didn't want to just do gay rooms, and working at Acme allowed me to find what was right for me."

Lee also made it a point to have Faris work with comics who would challenge her and make her better. "I remember he put me with Stanhope," Faris chuckles. "I was like, 'You can't put me with him! I'm a feminist! I can't handle it.' But he turned out to be the sweetest guy and a dear friend who would give you a million dollars if he had it. A lot of people broke those rules for me, and I needed it. Sabrina Matthews, Judy Gold, Kermet Apio: there was so much learning. You're so stupid when you get in this business. Acme is like a boot camp. Being with these people who were helpful and being around their creative brilliance was so fun to be a part of. I feel really lucky to have experienced all of that."

Tracey Ashley

Tracey Ashley got onstage at Acme for the first time in 1999, but it was definitely not the first time she had performed in front of a crowd. A former cruise director, Ashley was used to telling jokes and working an audience, but knew nothing about Acme before her first visit to the club. "I always wanted to be a comedian," she remembers. "I took classes at Stevie Ray's Comedy Cabaret for improv, and I saw that he had stand-up classes too. I took the class, worked on getting together three minutes of material, and one night we all went down to Acme."

In an example of pain and laughter going hand in hand, the day of her Acme debut Ashley broke up with her boyfriend, making the evening even more emotionally charged than it would have been if she'd just had a case of preshow jitters. "I went up there that night not knowing anything about the club, and it went fantastic," she recalls. "Laughter is the biggest

Tracey Ashley spent years finding her voice on the Acme stage. *Courtesy Acme Comedy Company*

The bond between comics Tracey Ashley and Pete Lee has remained strong even as their careers have grown. *Courtesy Acme Comedy Company*

drug ever. After I got off, Pete Lee came up to me and asked if I wanted to do comedy for real. I said yes, and he told me that I should keep coming back. That was all I needed to hear."

Though she was still finding her voice and looking for ways to dig deeper to develop her material, Ashley's charisma and energy made her stand out to Lee. Not that she knew that, however. "I was told not to talk to him," she laughs. "Pete came up to me one night and I said, 'Who's the owner of this place?' and he pointed at Louis, who was sitting in the back, and he goes, 'That's him right there.' So I said, 'Oh! I'm going to go talk to him!' And Pete goes, 'No, you can't talk to him! It'll ruin your career!'" The man whose coworkers berated him for not being an effective communicator when he first arrived in America was now an intimidating presence to comics who pride themselves on having big personalities onstage. But in reality, Lee chose to keep a distance from all of the comics to avoid any perceptions of favoritism. Still, that didn't mean he didn't enjoy making them squirm.

"I used to live in the Churchill Apartments, which were right up the street from Acme," Ashley recalls. "There used to be a little grocery store attached to my building. One time I went in to get some stuff, and I saw that Louis Lee was there. I saw him and my dumb ass walks up to him and says, 'Hi, I'm Tracey Ashley. I'm one of the comics who comes to your club. Thank you so much for letting me get up onstage.' And he just sort of nodded at me and kept moving. I ran out of that store faster than I've ever moved in my life."

Despite his unflinching poker face, Lee saw talent in Ashley and quietly made sure to provide opportunities to help her continue to develop. "Every Monday Louis would let me get on [stage]," she continues. "He was trying to create a community and create names among the comics. He would sit in the back of the club with a legal pad watching the open mic, which at the time I assumed was normal for comedy clubs. I didn't find out until later when I was on the road that the club owners were never taking notes or giving feedback. At one point, he watched everyone from his office. If he came out of his office to watch, you knew you were doing something right."

After Ashley spent months putting in her time and developing some solid material, the club gave her the green light to move up the ladder. "One of the managers came up to me one night and told me that they wanted to hire me as an emcee," she says. "At the time, I didn't realize what a big deal that was." Slowly, Lee and Ashley started to chat on a slightly more regular basis, and she quickly discovered that he wasn't the icy-cold presence she had originally imagined. "Louis ate it up," she laughs. "He would be laughing at how scared all of us comics were of him. He loved every minute of it. And I was so gullible that I'd believe anything he said, so he'd start messing with me. I'd be sitting in the bar, and he'd run in and yell at me, 'The headliner is almost done!' And I'd spill my drink all over myself running from the bar to the showroom, and the headliner would be nowhere near done. He was a prankster."

While he may have enjoyed picking on her, Lee was focused on helping Ashley elevate herself as a performer. "Louis told me that the funniest person isn't always the person who is already amazing," she recalls. "It's who has the most potential. That's who they really got behind." Similar to other comics on the scene at the time, Ashley bounced back and forth between Acme and Knuckleheads, gaining more confidence and a stronger stage presence. Despite her increased visibility, however, Ashley admits that her material began to stagnate.

"I remember one week Louis booked me to open for a comic named Ted Alexandro from New York," she says. "And after like two or three shows together, he asked me, 'Why don't you try some new material this week?' And I would say, 'Because it's going to suck.' He told me that you can't kill with the same material every single time, and it wasn't like the audience was going to eat me. So the next night I got up and did new material, and it bombed. And I walked off and Ted came up to me and said, 'Come back and do it again next week. Just make sure you have one solid joke in there to keep the audience and build around that.'"

Lee made it a point, as he did with some of the other up-and-comers, to put Ashley in lineups with comics who he thought could share helpful advice. "Tom Papa was really great. He talked to me a lot about consistency," she says. "Nick Swardson was great. He really believed in female comics. One night Steven Wright showed up unannounced and told me, 'Don't give me a big intro.' So I just said, 'Our next comic is from somewhere in Delaware. Give it up for Steven Wright.' The room went silent: they didn't think they heard me correctly until he walked out and the place went crazy. Jackie Kashian, Dwight York, John DeBoer. So many really great people. I remember one night he [Lee] had me opening for somebody, and told me that I should offer to take them around to see the town. I went in the green room and said, 'Can I take you on a tour of the city?' and he goes, 'If you want advice, just ask.' So I said, 'I would like some advice, please.' And he told me that I was very funny, but that I needed to dig deeper and talk about what I really cared about onstage. I think Louis wanted to tell me that same thing, but he thought it would mean more coming from a comic."

As time went on, Ashley became increasingly confident in her abilities, and felt she was ready to move up in the Acme hierarchy. Lee, however, had other plans. "Louis was so hard on me," she recalls. "I'd be so mad and in my feelings. I would get calls for TV shows or showcases, and he would tell me, 'You're not ready.' And I would be upset, but the thing is, he was right. Louis was tough, but it was because he wanted me to have more material. He used to say that a comic needed to be overprepared before they made that leap. He told me, 'I want you to be undeniable by the time [you] go out to LA or New York.' I would be coming offstage like, *I've got this*, and he'd tell me I wasn't ready to move up. It took me forever to become a feature, and it took me forever to eventually headline. But by the time I was ready to do colleges or headline on the road, I had the time I needed to be ready for it. I was more than ready. I had a real act. All because Louis was like, 'Nuh-uh. You keep writing. You don't have the time yet.' "

In addition to sharing advice about how to grow her career, Lee had also been around the industry long enough to offer valuable life advice to comics like Ashley who were on the precipice of comedy stardom. "He'd tell me, 'Don't make comedy your lifestyle.' That advice kept me grounded. He was right, because if you're not careful you can get so wrapped up in comedy and the road and the party, and he had seen that and didn't want that for me. He was right when he told me that you need to be overly ready, and it turned out he didn't just mean that about the material."

• • •

Though Lee was focused on helping this new group of comics prepare for what comedy would be like beyond their home club, he also befriended some comics who were considered too opinionated and strong-willed to fit in with the unspoken rules of the industry. Much like Lee himself, these individuals were misfits and outcasts of an art form that prides itself on uniqueness. And much like he had created an atmosphere for aspiring comics to find their voices, he opened his doors—and his stage—to those who weren't embraced in other clubs throughout the country.

Not only did Lee provide these individuals with a place to speak their minds freely, he also worked with them to raise those voices on the biggest platform possible.

• CHAPTER 6 •

POLITICALLY INCORRECT

Tim Slagle knew early on that he and Louis Lee were going to be friends. He also knew that not everyone appreciated his politics. "I started working at Acme because Becky [Johnson] thought I was cute," Slagle laughs. "The Hansens didn't find me funny, but Acme did, so I started coming twice a year." A Chicago-based comedian whom the *Star Tribune* once, early on in his career, called "a Libertarian Lenny Bruce," Slagle loved to push the audience. Whether that meant challenging people's political beliefs, bucking gender norms, or taking the contradictory stance on, well, pretty much anything liberals were on board with, Slagle's comedy was just as polarizing as it was funny.

Acme had been around for only a year when Slagle first arrived on the scene, but he felt comfortable there, even with his unique brand of comedy. "I found a home," he continues. "The Acme crowd was so nice that even if they didn't find you funny, they'd make you feel welcome." That welcoming attitude was put to the test one night when Johnson raised a concern with Lee over one of Slagle's jokes. "Becky loved my act until I started doing a bit about guys named Richard who will call themselves Dick, but women named Constance will never shorten their names beyond Connie," he recalls with a laugh. "She went and told Louis that she couldn't book me anymore.

Yes, that's his real hair. A dreadlocked Tim Slagle in his early Acme days. *Courtesy Jen Bryce*

He said he wanted to see the bit, so he came out of the back for the next show and watched me. He said there was nothing wrong with the bit, and I've been coming back every year for over thirty years."

Lee himself identifies as a political conservative, though he maintains that his personal beliefs have never influenced who he would or wouldn't allow to perform at his club. Other political comics, from Bobcat Goldthwait to Wyatt Cenac, have also found a platform at Acme to share their opinions, but no one has done it quite like Slagle. "I couldn't do my act anywhere," Slagle continues. "I always had trouble. The targets I picked for my jokes were the people who like to write letters. But Acme didn't care."

Slagle's antics weren't limited only to words, however. Over the years (and with Lee's blessing) he pulled stunts that no sane business owner would ever approve of. In the early 1990s, Slagle would close his performances with a joke that ended with him burning an American flag onstage. Sort of. "It was a pretty simple bit. Honestly, it was barely comedy," Slagle explains. "What I would do is I'd come onstage and bring out this tiny little flag and hold up a lighter. I'd explain that it wasn't a real flag because it had forty-seven stars and fourteen stripes. It was a Tim Slagle imitation flag made in China. So I'd have this flag, and I'd talk a little bit about how people felt about the flag, and then I'd have this little antenna in a lunchbox that would unfurl a copy of the Bill of Rights. I'd tell them that this [Bill of Rights] was what gave me the right to burn this flag. Then I'd light it, and it would be a little piece of flash paper that would go up immediately and everyone would ooh and ahh. It was more of a magic trick. But this was before the internet, so when comics saw me do it, they would tell club owners, 'Slagle is burning a flag onstage!' and the club owners would think that I was torching a full-sized flag, black tar dripping off of it, setting off smoke alarms. When that got out, I started losing bookings."

Slagle did the joke a handful of times at Acme, and while Lee would allow him to express himself however he saw fit, Louis also recognized that Slagle was doing damage to his own livelihood. "That killed his career," Lee says. "There was no tape or internet out there, so word of mouth was all you had to go off of. He lost a ton of work from that."

The flag burning stunt wasn't the last of Slagle's shenanigans. To this day, he holds the record for the most audience members walked (comedy-speak for causing a crowd to leave the show early) in a single show. "There are two separate times that I've walked an entire crowd," Slagle says proudly. "The last time I did it was when Paul Wellstone died in the middle of a Senate campaign. I came up with a line that I thought was really funny. They nominated Walter Mondale to be his replacement, and I'd say, 'Isn't he dead too?' So the first night I tried that onstage, it was a special Sunday night show, and it did great. The next night I did it at the open mic, and it had a great response there too. The next night I went out and opened with that line, and it was dead silence. At that point it was pretty clear Mondale was going to lose spectacularly, and the audience really just didn't find me amusing. I tried to bring them back, but after about fifteen minutes I could tell it wasn't going to work, so I chased them off. After that, Louis had to put up signs and warnings on the doors about how Acme supports free speech and how people aren't always going to enjoy everything that they hear."

Then there was the smoking protest. In 2007, the State of Minnesota enacted a smoking ban that included all bars, restaurants, and entertainment venues. Acme already had a no smoking policy in the showroom and the restaurant, but up until then smoking had been allowed in the bar. Recognizing that the new rule could potentially hurt his business, Lee wasn't happy with the change. "In the early days, Louis would let the young kids [audience members under the age of twenty-one] smoke in the showroom during the open mic night, as a way to keep them in the club," Slagle recalls. "So he was really mad, because a third of his business is reserved for smokers. At that point in my career, I used to perform onstage with a lit cigarette because it was part of my stage character. And the way the law was written, you could smoke onstage as long as it was part of the performance. So I suggested we stage a protest."

Never one to shy away from pushing the envelope, Lee was on board with the plan immediately. "My idea was that we would set up police tape way out into the audience, and say that it was part of my stage. My performance was called, 'Smoking in a comedy club,'" Slagle continues. "Louis thought it was great. He got a documentarian who was going to film it, sent out press releases, news stations showed up. We even had protestors from the Lung Association."

After his initial stunt, Slagle began incorporating the bit into his act. "I'd make a big deal about the law and the fact that I could smoke onstage but the audience couldn't smoke,"

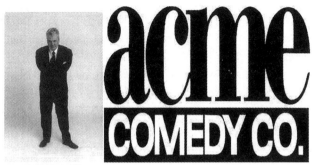

acme
COMEDY CO.

TIM SLAGLE

PRESS ALERT: FOR IMMEDIATE RELEASE

SMOKE ALARM!

Like to laugh and light up a cig?

Tim says, "Bring your butts to Acme"

SMOKERS INVITED - ONE NIGHT ONLY: Thurs., Nov. 3 8pm

***** During Tim's set, he'll invite you to smoke. When he does, go ahead and light up.*****

(Beware – you may be caught on tape – an Academy Award winning film team will be taping for "Devil's Weed" – a doc about smoking bans)

Nationally acclaimed headlining comedian and political pundit **Tim Slagle** is pushing the envelope, expanding the borders of the stage to incorporate what some clubs used to call a 'smoking section'.

Acme Comedy Company is giving free reign to Mr. Slagle. He's requested that the audience be seated by smoking preference. Acme has not allowed smoking in the club for years (except in the bar, in the good old days). But Tim has earned his Artistic License. Our stage will expand to include Tim's special section of social outcasts – the smokers.

So, on Tim's behalf, we are spreading the word. Smokers, come on down. Tim will bring the ash trays.

TV credits: the usual cable TV comedy shows, C-SPAN, news/politics TV nationwide Liberty Magazine, contributing editor

Contact: Angie Piche (612) 338-6393 Photos, more info available at **timslagle.com**

TICKETS: $15 (show only) DINNER/SHOW PACKAGE: $27

708 1st Street North Warehouse District, Minneapolis acmecomedycompany.com (612) 338-6393

A flyer for Tim Slagle's indoor smoking protest at Acme in the mid-2000s. *Courtesy Jen Bryce*

he remembers. "So I'd say, 'Do you want to smoke?' and bring some chairs onstage and call it the smoking section, and people would watch the rest of my show from the stage and smoke." Much like the flag burning joke years earlier, word got out about his stunt. Only this time, his audience was far more open to his antics. "People would wait for me to open up the smoking section onstage and ask to be the ones who got to come up. It was always big fun."

The big fun got out of hand, however, and for the first—and only—time in their history together, Lee had to tell Slagle to kill the bit. "Louis comes up to me after a show one night and goes, 'You're still doing that smoking bit?' And I said, 'Yes, I am.' He goes, 'I heard someone pulled out a joint tonight and lit it onstage.' I kind of laughed and said, 'I did think that cigarette smelled a little funny,'" Slagle recalls, still giggling at the interaction years later. "So he just says, 'I think that bit is hack now.' Which was his way of telling me not to do it. That's the only time he ever asked me not to do something onstage."

From the early days of controversy (and maybe because of them), Slagle and Lee formed a friendship. And from that friendship emerged an exceedingly ambitious political offering (at least for a comedy bit): Mudslingers Ball. "Louis and I used to hang out after shows," Slagle says. "We'd stay up all night drinking and come up with crazy ideas. I pitched him the idea of a political debate show, and he liked it." The concept was simple: put two comedians onstage who had starkly differing political views and let them have at each other. Then, throw in some live audience questions and comments, to achieve the *Jerry Springer* car crash–style TV that was insanely popular at the time. Finally, follow a loose scorekeeping system, and declare a winner at the end of the show. The idea was innovative in a time when traditional stand-up was at its most stale.

"[If you were a comic] you were only supposed to have one opinion politically at that time," Slagle recalls. "I've always been antiauthoritarian, and I felt like at that point the people on the left were actually embracing a lot of the ideas that [they] had typically been opposed to, because they worked in their favor."

The stage was set for, fittingly, Fourth of July week 1997 at Acme. On the right, you had Slagle. His opponent on the left was a West Coast–based comic named James Inman. And playing the emcee and referee for the evening was Minnesota comedy legend Alex Cole. They had the players and the structure, but getting people to understand their vision was a different matter. "A lot of people showed up just expecting a comedy show," Slagle says. "Again, this was before the internet, so it was hard to promote it and tell people what we were going to do." A review in the *Star Tribune* by comedy writer Colin Covert didn't do the show any favors, taking the political experiment to task after the very first night. "The idea of a comic debate is an intriguing idea, but Tuesday's opening night fell far short of its potential," Covert wrote. "There were moments of political insight, but they weren't side-splitting. There were laughs, but they weren't based on exposing grand ideological idiocies."

To their credit, Slagle and Inman stayed unflinchingly committed to the format. Slagle commented on everything from the repercussions of Hong Kong being handed over to China to his belief that the government should be trimmed back to the few areas where it had a proven record of competence, like sewage removal. Inman held his ground as well, raging over the idea that McDonald's restaurants could keep their restrooms off-limits to noncustomers.

Initial reviewers may have been lukewarm on the concept, but the show found an audience, and Slagle brought the Ball back to Acme several times after that. It did so well, in fact, that in 2000, Slagle and Lee decided to kick things up a notch by filming the show with the intent to sell it to a broadcast network. But to translate the act to TV, the show needed to be bigger. That meant a more grandiose production, and more comedians to hurl jabs at one another. "Lewis Black was just about to pop," says Slagle. "We knew everyone would come in to see him. The thing I liked about Lewis was that he appreciated that I would offer counter opinions to him. Even when he started doing more media interviews talking about political comedy, he would refer the reporters to me if they wanted to hear the other side."

Along with Black, Acme decided to bring in political satirist Will Durst to stack the left side of the political scales. Durst, a Wisconsin native, was already an Acme favorite by that time, and his role as the host of the PBS series *Livelyhood* amplified his star power. Meanwhile, conservative comic Jeff Jena would come in to join Slagle in fending off their big shot political opponents. It was a perfect mix of personalities and politics, all the ingredients for making great television. The pilot taping was scheduled for early March, with plans of turning it around for TV stations shortly thereafter. While they had the talent and the concept, Lee and the rest of the team quickly realized they needed some additional help on the production side of things. Once again, Lee looked to his friends.

Rich Miller agreed to come in as a partner on the project, and former manager Jennifer Bryce was willing to serve as a producer. But according to Bryce, the project was the blind leading the blind. "They had the guys committed and a time to shoot it, but they didn't have a showrunner to help pull it together," she says. "Louis called me and asked me to do it. He offered me 10 percent in the project, but didn't want me telling Rich and Tim that he had promised me a slice." Bryce sprang into action the week of the event, setting up production, lighting, and talent management, all while butting heads with her newfound partners. "The show was Tim's idea, but he felt intimidated by the people who had agreed to do it [Black and Durst]," she says. "So I literally spent the week running around pulling everything together, and Louis hasn't told anybody why I'm here. People are looking at me like, *We didn't know Jen was involved in this.*"

Her responsibilities went beyond producing and show running. "Lewis Black came up to me the day of the show and said, 'I hope you found a good makeup artist.' I told him that we had a shoestring budget, so he would have to do his own.

He told me that he wasn't going out in front of a camera without a decent makeup artist, so I had like two hours to track someone down. Luckily, my friend Beatrice who ran Fashion Week was around, so she agreed to come in and do it, so Lewis was happy. But when other people saw me bringing in friends and telling people what to do, it really annoyed them."

Hiccups and production headaches aside, the taping was a success. Now they just needed to find someone to put it on the air. "KSTP [the local ABC affiliate in Minneapolis] picked up the show the next month," Slagle recalls. "They put us on Saturday night, and we actually came in second locally, behind *SNL* but ahead of *MADtv*." The wheels were spinning, and it looked like big things were in store for the show. Slagle and Lee envisioned a broader focus for the Ball moving forward, with teams that brought female and minority perspectives to the table, along with new topics of debate. "You could have fat guys who loved sandwiches against girls who eat only salads," laughs Slagle. "I wanted to keep it political, but the point was that it could be flexible depending on where we went." The following month, it was announced that Mudslingers Ball would visit Slagle's hometown of Chicago as part of the Chicago Comedy Festival, with the same foursome doing battle. The Ball was going on the road.

Back at home, the show had outperformed network expectations, and KSTP was interested in having more episodes produced. "They didn't hit our number," Slagle says, explaining how the station failed to meet the crew's asking price for more of the televised mud battle. "In retrospect, we should have taken advantage of that, found some investors, and tried to make something of it." Once it became clear they would part ways with KSTP, Bryce asked if she could take a stab at shopping the show somewhere else. "We created this really brilliant show," she remembers. "And Louis was the spider at the center of it. So after it got some attention locally, Rich Miller said he was going to try and sell it somewhere else. When he couldn't,

I asked if I could take it, and I was told, 'No, that's Rich's territory.' At that point I was mad at Louis, everyone was mad at me, and it just sort of drifted away."

To their credit, Miller, Slagle, and Lee did take it to Hollywood and screened the show for a handful of network executives. "They told us that it was interesting, but that they didn't want to do a Minnesota show," recalls Slagle. "But wouldn't you know it? Six months later there were a couple of shows on their networks that were nearly identical." One of the original concept's stars wound up hosting one of these new shows. "He might admit it, I don't know," Slagle says reluctantly. "But basically Lewis Black took our show and it became *Root of All Evil*."

Root of All Evil was on the air for less than a year in 2008, and featured Black playing moderator while two comics debated a variety of topics. Andy Kindler and Paul F. Tompkins clashed over the NRA and PETA; Greg Giraldo and Kathleen Madigan sparred on strip clubs and sororities; Andy Daly and Patton Oswalt debated Las Vegas and the human body. The show received mixed reviews from critics but was a hit with viewers. While Black has never gone on record to say that he based the show on Mudslingers Ball, the similarities are certainly evident. In fact, one of the original mudslingers, James Inman, still boasts on his website, "co-creator of Mudslingers Ball, which later became Lewis Black's *Root of All Evil*."

Though the show never resurfaced locally, Slagle and Lee's bond has continued to grow stronger, with Slagle still coming back to Acme every year. "Louis has always told me, 'I've been right about every comic who I've ever said was going to make it big—except for you,'" Slagle laughs. "Maybe that's why he keeps letting me try things and get away with so much. He doesn't want to be wrong." No matter Slagle's career fortunes, Acme will always be a place that is willing to take risks and provide a stage for comics to share their beliefs, even if it ends with two hundred people leaving the club before the show is over. "I love coming to Acme because I can push it there," Slagle says. "Before my week there every year I go through my old notebooks and find the stuff I can't do anywhere else anymore, because I know there's an audience for it at Acme."

Lee is guarded when it comes to his relationships with comics, and was even more so back in his early days. But his connection with the local comics was always much deeper than business, and that depth allowed him to quietly beam with pride over their success. Unfortunately, Lee would soon learn that that connection could also result in a great deal of pain, frustration, and sadness.

• CHAPTER 7 •

THE LAMP

As at most comedy clubs, the green room at Acme is nothing to write home about. It's got a couple of busted-up couches, a coffee table that looks like it wouldn't fetch ten dollars at a garage sale, and more marks, dings, and nicks in the walls than you can count. In the corner sits a small desk lamp. It's the most unremarkable piece of furniture in the entire room, and looks like it was stolen out of a budget hotel. Which it was. By Mitch Hedberg.

"The last time Mitch ever came in here [Acme], it was when him and Lewis Black recorded albums with Comedy Central back-to-back," recalls Lee. "He was huge at that point. Both of them were. That week, Mitch told me that the fluorescent lights in the green room were bothering his eyes. The next night, I came in and he had stolen the lamp from his hotel and put it back there." Those album-recording shows took place at Acme in May 2003. Less than two years later, Hedberg was dead.

Though he was originally from St. Paul, it feels a little dishonest to call Hedberg a Minnesota comic. After graduating from high school in 1986, he decided to move to Fort Lauderdale, Florida, where he got his first taste of stand-up, despite a horrible case of stage fright. Eventually he moved to Seattle, where he continued pursuing comedy, before finally making his way back home in 1993, when he began picking up regular road gigs from Scott Hansen, while trying to get up wherever else he could find stage time. Including at Acme. "The first time he performed at Acme, Becky [Johnson] hired him to be a feature," says Lee. "And people *hated* him. Half of the audience went and waited in the bar for him to be done before they would come back in."

Doug Stanhope, who became close friends with Hedberg, had a similar experience the first time he watched Mitch perform in Minnesota. "I met him at Knuckleheads," says Stanhope. "It was me and Louis Johnson, a Black guy out of Denver, and then Mitch was the emcee. He got up and died his ass off, except for me and Louis, who loved him." As anyone familiar with Hedberg's brand of offbeat, one-liner comedy can attest, he had a style that was completely unique. The problem, Stanhope says, is that bookers were still trying to put him into conventional comedy club roles. "Hedberg is not a fucking emcee," he laughs. "Can you picture that guy telling you the drink specials for the night?"

Dave Mordal also had the chance to work with Hedberg at Scott Hansen's Comedy Gallery early in his career, and recognized the potential he had once the audience grasped what the heck he was doing onstage. "I mean, he was just killing me, but the rest of the audience wasn't getting it at all," he shared in a *Star Tribune* feature about Hedberg following his death. "I knew that once he figured out how to make the audience get it, he would be unstoppable."

Eventually the crowds caught up, and an appearance on the *Late Show with David Letterman* in 1996 firmly cemented Hedberg's role as a bona fide headliner and star on the rise. And while he got plenty of headlining work locally at the Comedy Gallery, Medina Entertainment Center, and Knuckleheads, he was still sparsely used at Acme until mid-1997, when Jennifer Bryce had taken over booking duties at the club. "He was such a decent guy whose brain worked inside out and backwards,"

Bryce recalls. "But he wasn't reliable because of his drug use." The only thing equally synonymous with Hedberg as his monotone delivery style was his well-publicized drug habits. Onstage, he'd make light of his use ("I used to do drugs. I still do, but I used to, too" he'd say in one of his most quotable bits), but offstage his life imitated his art.

"Most of the stuff Mitch did back then was based in truth," explains Stanhope. "One night at Acme I remember he made a joke about how you can try a new version of something, and then the original is never as good again. He said something like, 'Have you ever smoked weed with a little bit of heroin? You can't go back.' And I'm sitting in the back like, *Huh. That line was a midweek add.* So that night after the show we're in the green room doing coke, and I said, 'Hey was that line about heroin for real?' And he just looks at me and says, 'I have no plans of slowing down.'" Hedberg certainly didn't slow down, and neither did his ascent to comedy superstardom. A show-stealing performance at the 1998 Just for Laughs Comedy Festival in Montreal led executives from Fox television network to sign him to an unprecedented half-million-dollar deal to develop a sitcom. *Time* magazine anointed him "the next Seinfeld" thanks to his clever observations and one-of-a-kind delivery.

Hedberg was on top of the comedy world. In 1999, he performed a weekend of co-headlining shows at Acme alongside Stanhope, which became one of the most legendary performances in the club's history. "They just kept going," laughs Bryce. "I think they stayed onstage until something like 2 A.M. Everyone got caught up in it. They were just riffing and upping the insanity. It would get to a point where you thought they couldn't possibly keep going, but they did." The same year, Hedberg wrote and directed his own film, *Los Enchiladas!* It told the story of a group of Mexican restaurant employees in St. Paul, modeled after his own experiences working at Chi-Chi's at Maplewood Mall. Alongside Hedberg, the film starred soon-to-be-household names like Dave Attell, Marc Maron, and Todd Barry. Unfortunately, the film fell flat. It screened a handful of times at festivals and one-night-only celebrations, but was never picked up for any type of wider distribution.

Though Hedberg's acting career wasn't taking off, his rise in comedy continued, both in Minnesota and across the country. Hedberg performed regularly in the Twin Cities, though he had by then made the leap to theaters as opposed to clubs. A follow-up appearance at the Just for Laughs Festival in 2001 solidified him as one of the hottest comedians in the country—and a true "comic's comic," which essentially meant he was someone who entertained and inspired other comics.

But the drugs were still there. Hedberg's use continued at a blistering pace, and in late 2001 he gave an interview to *Penthouse* magazine with an eerie foreshadow of what was to come. "If you could choose, how would your life end?" he was asked. Without missing a beat, he responded, "First, I'd want to get famous, and then I'd overdose. If I overdosed at this stage of my career, I would be lucky if it made the back pages."

In the late spring of 2003, Hedberg decided to record his sophomore album at what had become his home club: Acme. The album recording shows were a hot ticket for local comedy lovers, many of whom had only recently discovered the comedy gem that had been hidden right under their noses for many years. One of those fans was Kevin Estling. A diehard comedy fan and open micer, Estling had begun listening to Hedberg's stuff when he was a college student, and credited Hedberg with opening his eyes and ears to a new generation of comedians. Estling was an Acme regular, whether he was just hanging out or getting up casually at the weekly open mic. "Everyone was so cool back then," he recalls. "That's what I loved about it. I'd be like a fly on the wall hanging around the comics at Acme, just thinking, *These guys are so funny!*"

When he heard the news of Hedberg recording at Acme, Estling knew he had to be there. "We got tickets for the 10:30

show that Saturday night, and I was outside smoking while the host was onstage," Estling recalls. "Mitch came walking in, he was stumbling a little bit, but at that point I just said something like, 'Have a great show.' He smiled, and I figured, *Hey, I got to say hello to Mitch Hedberg! That's pretty cool.*" After the show, Estling was in the bar as Hedberg made his way out from the green room. "I went up to him and wanted to talk about *Los Enchiladas!* because I had heard there was a VHS copy going around the club," he says. "I told him that I wanted to see it because I had heard it was really funny, which was a lie because everyone told me it was awful."

Hedberg seemed genuinely excited to meet someone who cared about his creative endeavors beyond the mainstream projects. He zeroed in on Estling and struck up a conversation. "He talked to me for probably fifteen or twenty minutes," recalls Estling. "He's being polite if people say hello, but it really seemed like he was just ignoring everyone and was focused on me. The most interesting part was that he really didn't want to talk about himself. He kept asking me questions about where I grew up. I remember I told him I was from Fridley, and he goes, 'Oh man. Friendly Fridley. That was dumb. I'm sorry.' He told me some stories about growing up in Maplewood while the rest of the bar was clearing out. It was sort of surreal that I didn't just get to meet Mitch, but he was hanging out and such a caring person."

Hedberg eventually gave his new pals a Minnesota goodbye, apologizing profusely as he left the club. But the night wasn't over just yet. "Me and my buddies are all amped up after that, and they make a last call at the bar, so we decide to have one more. About twenty minutes later the club is closed and we're finishing our drinks at a high-top table, and I look up and here comes Mitch stumbling back down the stairs into the club. He walks over to me and goes, 'Hey I want to get your address so I can send you a copy of *Los Enchiladas!*' I gave it to him, but I never got the movie."

The following month, Hedberg was arrested at the airport in Austin, Texas, for heroin possession, when a routine security check of his carry-on bag revealed large sums of cash—Hedberg at that point was asking for his payout from shows to be provided in cash—along with three syringes and a can of Red Bull that tested positive for heroin. While he was being processed at the local jail, authorities discovered that his right leg had become severely infected because of needle injections. It was so bad, in fact, that doctors believed gangrene had started to occur and the leg would need to be amputated. Fortunately, after six weeks in the hospital and a surgical procedure where muscle from his back was grafted into the damaged area, doctors saved the leg and Mitch was able to get back on his feet—both of them.

For the next six months, Hedberg disappeared from performing to work on his physical recovery from the surgery, as well as on his sobriety. Lee, who hadn't had much contact with Hedberg since his album recording earlier in the year, was relieved to hear that the young comic was focused on getting healthy. Which made it all the more infuriating when he learned Hedberg was going right back on the road that winter alongside Dave Attell and Lewis Black.

"Dave Becky with 3 Arts was Mitch's manager, and he also managed Attell and Lewis Black," Lee recalls. "I heard he had put the tour together, and I was furious. Lewis and Dave had a reputation as guys who loved to drink and party. How can you put him on the road with two guys who want to do that all the time and expect him to stay clean? I actually ran into Lewis Black at a wedding before the tour started and told him I was worried about Mitch. He said they would do their best to give him space and not let him get into any trouble, but I knew there was nothing he could do. After that, I refused to work with Dave Becky for a long time." Hedberg managed to finish the whirlwind tour, opening for Black and Attell on each of their forty-four nationwide shows, while maintaining his sobriety. With plans for another headlining tour the following year, it looked like the kid whom early Acme crowds couldn't stand was going to get his redemption arc after all. Then came Just for Laughs.

In what should have been a full-circle moment, the festival invited Hedberg back to the place where he had first taken the industry by storm six years earlier. Lee and Bryce had become regulars at the festival, attending each year to scout new talent and build industry connections. When they saw Hedberg was on the bill for 2004, it became a top priority to see how he was keeping on. "Mitch was doing two shows that weekend," recalls Bryce. "The big show was open to the public at 7, and then there was an industry-only show at midnight. Louis and I went to the first show, and he was incredible. Just absolutely brilliant. You could see that he'd been through treatment, and he seemed like he was the best he'd ever been. Sometime between that show and the midnight show he had fallen off the wagon. He came out onstage for the late show, laid down on the stage, and just started mumbling into the microphone until they escorted him off the stage. All I could do was sit there and cry." That night was the last time Lee and Bryce saw the comic alive.

On March 30, 2005, Hedberg was found dead in his hotel room in New Jersey, the result of an accidental drug overdose. He was just thirty-seven years old. A collective sense of grief gripped fans and comics alike. Everyone from Conan O'Brien to George Carlin penned tributes to Hedberg in the weeks and months that followed, cementing the impact he had made in comedy. But for Hedberg's longtime friend Doug Stanhope, his death symbolized something much scarier. "When he died, I was surprised," Stanhope recalls. "Me and my girlfriend at the time were crying, but we said that we weren't crying for Mitch. We were crying for ourselves, because he was the first person to make us realize we're mortal."

While those who admired Hedberg's comedy were upset

by the news of his passing, no one was as devastated as his parents. "This was a guy with plans," his father, Arne, said in a *Star Tribune* interview. "He always had ideas. He didn't want to die." The month following his death, a funeral was held for Hedberg at the St. Ambrose Catholic Church in Woodbury, Minnesota. Despite only having a brief connection to Mitch, Estling decided to attend the service. "I saw his mom [Mary Hedberg] walking down the aisle that day, and she was just a quivering mess," Estling recalls. "I just wanted to give her a hug so badly." Following the funeral, Estling and Hedberg's parents became close friends and collaborators. Estling helped the Hedbergs with fundraising efforts, like an annual golf tournament, to honor Mitch's memory while raising money for treatment facilities throughout Minnesota.

After a year of funerals, waves of media stories, and tributes from fellow comics, Arne and Mary decided they wanted to honor their son and his memory with a comedy show. "I got a call from Mitch's mother," Lee recalls. "She said that Mitch's

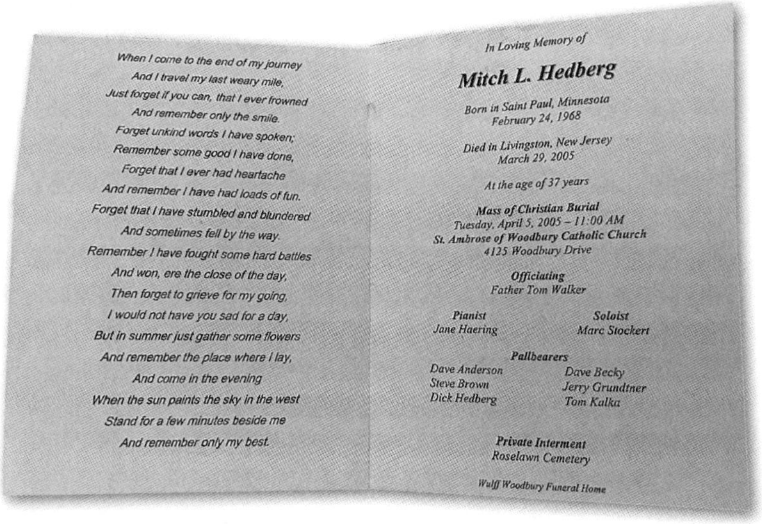

When I come to the end of my journey
And I travel my last weary mile,
Just forget if you can, that I ever frowned
And remember only the smile.
Forget unkind words I have spoken;
Remember some good I have done,
Forget that I ever had heartache
And remember I have had loads of fun.
Forget that I have stumbled and blundered
And sometimes fell by the way.
Remember I have fought some hard battles
And won, ere the close of the day,
Then forget to grieve for my going,
I would not have you sad for a day,
But in summer just gather some flowers
And remember the place where I lay,
And come in the evening
When the sun paints the sky in the west
Stand for a few minutes beside me
And remember only my best.

In Loving Memory of

Mitch L. Hedberg

Born in Saint Paul, Minnesota
February 24, 1968

Died in Livingston, New Jersey
March 29, 2005

At the age of 37 years

Mass of Christian Burial
Tuesday, April 5, 2005 – 11:00 AM
*St. Ambrose of **Woodbury Catholic Church***
4125 Woodbury Drive

Officiating
Father Tom Walker

Pianist *Jane Haering*
Soloist *Marc Stockert*

Pallbearers
Dave Anderson · *Dave Becky*
Steve Brown · *Jerry Grundtner*
Dick Hedberg · *Tom Kalka*

Private Interment
Roselawn Cemetery

Wulff Woodbury Funeral Home

Program from Mitch Hedberg's funeral in Woodbury, Minnesota, 2005.
Courtesy Kevin Estling

one-year anniversary was coming up, and his wife and a few comics want to do a show here at Acme. She said whatever money they made from the event they wanted to give to a charity they started in Mitch's honor. I told her no, because Mitch deserved a lot bigger." Instead of holding the event at the club, Lee decided the show would take place at the Orpheum Theatre in downtown Minneapolis.

When it came time to book the talent for the big event, he contacted his old friend Rich Miller, who gave Lee some tough love. "Rich told me, 'You have to reach out to Dave Becky and 3 Arts,'" Lee recalls. "[Rich] sat me down and said, 'Louis, you're wrong.' And I asked why, and he told me, 'Dave Becky can put together an offer for Mitch, but Mitch made the decision to take it. He was facing a lot of legal issues; he needed the money for lawyers.' And that's when I realized he was

Mitch Hedberg's friends and family, including Dave Attell, Todd Barry, Hedberg's widow Lynn Shawcroft, and many more, paying their respects during his tribute show, which was produced by Acme. *Courtesy Jen Bryce*

An autographed poster featuring some of comedy's biggest stars, in town for the Mitch Hedberg Memorial Show in 2006. *Courtesy Jen Bryce*

right." Lee swallowed his pride and buried the hatchet with Becky, who was equally motivated to make the show a success.

On April 30, 2006, the Mitch Hedberg Tribute sold out the Orpheum, with major headliners like Patton Oswalt, Todd Barry, Dave Attell, and Mike Birbiglia joining some of Hedberg's former Acme cohorts like Nick Swardson, Dave Mordal, and Tim Slagle. Even Hedberg's widow, Lynn Shawcroft, took the stage, for what was a massively successful and touching tribute to a comic who lost his life far too soon. "There were a lot of raw emotions that were still there," recalls Bryce of the show. "People were literally driving and flying from all over the country for this event. And for Louis to handle the tribute the way he did meant so much to Mitch's parents. And I think it meant a lot to Louis too."

· CHAPTER 8 ·

THE CURSE AND THE LOCK

The first summer Acme was open, the club hosted an amateur contest billed as "Acme's Funniest Person Contest." The FPC, as it would become known, shared a lot of similarities with other comedy contests at clubs throughout the country. It was a good way to bring in new customers. It offered amateur comics an opportunity to get stage time. And it awarded the winner a cash prize of a thousand dollars. Bryan Miller, a longtime Acme comic and onetime contest finalist (he came in fourth in 2009), hosts a podcast dedicated to the FPC, where he interviews past winners and contestants about their contest experiences. "A lot of places will do a contest in the summer instead of hosting an open mic," explains Miller. "Or they'll do it on an off night to bring people in. With those contests, you usually get a bunch of amateurs and then like ten minutes of a headliner."

Acme chose to present its contest differently. Instead of saving it for an off night, they included a small group of contestants during each show throughout the summer. While other clubs tried to get amateurs to bring friends who might buy a few drinks, Acme chose to allow contestants to bring friends who would see a full show, complete with the contest, then a feature, followed by a highly regarded headline act. Though the decision to mesh the contest with the "real"

Comedian Bryan Miller is an Acme headliner, host of *The Funniest Person Podcast*, and former contest fourth-place recipient. *Courtesy Acme Comedy Company*

shows is something that plenty of clubs would (and continue to) scoff at, Miller explains that Acme's decision made a lot of sense, and ultimately supported the goal of rebuilding the local comedy scene.

"It's genius business-wise," says Miller. "It fills so many functions. First, it gets new people interested in comedy. There are so many people who aren't sure how to get started [performing comedy], and the contest acclimates people who want to try it out. Plus they do it in the summer, which helps fill out the summer schedule, which is historically slower for comedy clubs. It's just a great targeted thing. You get maybe twelve to fifteen people per night who come in for free because they want to see their buddy from work or whatever and it's a free ticket, and they get to see a full show. Even if the contestants are terrible, you're going to get a solid opener and a national headliner. It's a win for everyone."

The other factor that sets Acme's FPC apart from the usual comedy contests, Miller says, is that it is truly an amateur contest. "Everyone gets three minutes," he explains. "It's always been that way since the beginning. And every round it's the same. I asked Louis one time why he doesn't do it like some contests, where the first round is three minutes, the next is five, and the finals are like seven. He told me, 'It's an *amateur* contest. If you start adding more and more time, then it starts being a professional thing. But with three minutes, anyone has a chance.' And that made so much sense to me."

By definition, if you've been paid to perform comedy, Acme no longer considers you an amateur and therefore won't allow you to enter the contest. The club and the comics have taken this rule seriously from the get-go as a way to uphold the contest's integrity. As Miller himself has seen, this rule isn't always observed at other clubs. "I did one contest where it was so clearly obvious who won," Miller explains. "Then they announced the winner, and it was some longtime comic who was friends with the booker and owed him some money, so he did that as a favor to make it up to him. That kind of shit happens all the time."

While there were checks in place to make sure comics weren't ringers, there were also no guarantees that the contestants themselves would be any good. That possibility went completely out the window the very first year of the contest, when Dave Mordal took home the title. "Dave Mordal is just so good," Miller says. "To have him win your first year sets the bar really high." Mordal was arguably the first truly homegrown Acme talent in the club's history, parlaying his win in 1992 into a decades-long comedy career that took him all over the country, and into Hollywood.

Aside from Mordal, the FPC produced a handful of winners like Rox Tarrant and Bill Rainey, who used the victory as a stepping stone to grow their comedy careers. But by the mid-nineties, an eerie trend began to develop within the contest. "There was

The very first Acme Funniest Person Contest winner, Dave Mordal.
Courtesy Acme Comedy Company

this jinx that people talked about," Chad Daniels told Miller during their episode of the FPC podcast. "You looked at the list of winners over the past few years, and none of them were doing comedy anymore. So in a way, it was almost like it was better not to win. Which I'm sure was just everyone who didn't win making an excuse so that they felt better." Daniels initially tried the contest in 1998, losing in the first round. The following year, after he had become a regular at the club, Daniels made the finals, ultimately finishing third. While Daniels himself took the loss in stride, another of his fellow contestants was less than gracious in defeat. "There was a guy in a cow costume who got so indignant that he didn't win that he threw his gift card that he got on the floor and stormed off the stage," Daniels laughs. "So I grabbed his gift card and got two that night."

Jinx or not, the reality was that plenty of wannabe comics throughout Acme's first decade seemed to be satisfied to cross stand-up comedy off of their bucket lists, cash their prize checks, and move on with their lives. Then in the early 2000s, things changed. In 2002, a woman named Elaine Cory (Elaine Thompson at the time) from Farmington won the annual comedy battle royal. The thirty-seven-year-old attorney was the true definition of amateur, as she had tried only a few open mics before her impressive run through the competition. "When I won I looked at my husband and was sort of like, *Oh, well that's cool. Alright let's go home*," Cory laughs, reflecting on her big win. "That night, Louis Lee came up to me and said he wanted me to start coming to the club on Mondays, and that I didn't need to sign up," she recalls. "He told me to just call and tell them I was coming, and they would put me on the list. I didn't realize what a huge deal that really was."

Cory came in to Acme during a period of transition in the local talent pool. The previous comedy class that included folks like Pete Lee and Tracey Ashley had graduated to emcee and feature-level performers. But unlike those groups, who all started around the same time and came up the ranks together, Cory was something of a lone wolf. "Tracey [Ashley] told me that it had sort of become a tradition that someone would win the contest and then never be heard from ever again," she recalls. "So she was excited to see I was sticking around."

Acme soon hired Cory as an emcee. Despite the initial encouragement from Lee, she says she found herself somewhat scared of her new employer. "Someone told me early on that I wasn't supposed to talk to Louis," she says. "I didn't know that when I started, but once I heard that and realized none of the other comics would talk to him at the open mic night or during shows, I was kind of scared of him." Despite being intimidated by Lee, Cory says he was always supportive of her and her material, which tended to be darker and dirtier than some of Acme's other comics. "I didn't want to do stuff about women's issues," she says. "I would do stuff that was dirty. I remember the first time I emceed at Acme, I opened for Emo Philips. He came up to me before the show and said, 'OK, go clean. Don't do anything dirty.' And I had to let him know that I didn't have any material that was clean. He was really pissed about that, but Louis spent a lot of time talking to him and he backed me up to make sure I could do the stuff that worked for me."

Cory worked at Acme for the next couple of years, though she never progressed beyond club emcee. By her own admission, the reason was simply that she wasn't willing to take chances onstage, which is what Lee was interested in seeing. "I had material that worked and I knew it," she says. "I was too terrified to try new material. If I tried new stuff and it didn't get a huge laugh, I'd lean on my old stuff. So I wasn't really progressing, and then Acme stopped booking me as much. Then they started making me sign up for open mic, and I decided to go put my energy elsewhere."

Though she didn't end up following in the footsteps of people like Tracey Ashley, Cory says she became a much better comic thanks to the club, and of course, she broke the jinx. "Acme helped me get into better clubs and better gigs than I would have done on my own," she says plainly. "People come to Acme and learn how to be an audience member at a show, and they know what to expect." Before she left Acme, Cory served as the emcee for the FPC finals in 2003, when Acme's most famous love story began onstage.

Tim Harmston and Mary Mack have been happily married for over twenty years. But in 2003, they were two comics competing with two very different motivations. "I had been doing stand-up since March of 2002," Harmston recalled during his turn on the FPC podcast. "So I had about fourteen or fifteen months of experience, but I wasn't getting up at Acme. I'd show up every Monday for the open mic, and they weren't putting me on." While Harmston was trying to get the club to give him a closer look as he worked his way up the comedy ladder, Mack just needed the money. "I had a polka band in Nashville, and we had been down there recording our album,"

Mack recalls. "Don't worry—it didn't go anywhere. Anyways, I was in Minnesota and I saw an ad in the *City Pages* that you could win money in this comedy contest. I needed the money to get back to Nashville and finish that album, so I signed up."

Despite different motivations, both Harmston and Mack

Married couple Tim Harmston and Mary Mack onstage at the club where they first met in 2003, Acme Comedy Company. *Courtesy Acme Comedy Company*

advanced through the competition that summer. For Harmston, it was thanks to thoroughly workshopped material that he'd crafted and worked on at other open mics around town. For Mack, it was something else altogether. "I'd get up and write my jokes that morning that I wanted to do that night," Mack laughs. "That's how I did it. I didn't know you could do it another way. Those three minutes were so bad. I think people just felt sorry for me. I don't know if they were sympathy-laughing or laughing because it was so absurd, but they were kind to me." Whatever the reason, Mack was getting laughs and advancing through the summer. Even when others tried to offer helpful advice, she wouldn't listen. "Mindy, who was the club manager at the time, told me, 'You know, you can come here on open mic night to practice and try out your set.' And I just thought, *Why would I do that? I want to be fresh for the show.* I did not understand comedy at all."

Eventually, the two crossed paths at the club, sizing each other up. "I told my friend Catherine that I had a crush on him because he had, like, cool seventies hair," Mack says of her initial reaction to Harmston. "But I also saw that he was doing the same set every time, and I was like, *Hey that's cheating!* Both Harmston and Mack made it to the finals that year, with Harmston ultimately winning the competition. "One time Tim went up to my friend and said, 'You know, Mary got robbed. She should have come in second,'" Mack recalls.

After winning the big competition, Harmston was riding high on what he believed to be his key to the Acme kingdom, and he celebrated that way. "I won the contest, and it was a big party at the club that night," he remembers. "The manager came up to me and asked if I wanted to go on the radio the next morning with the headliner—who was Will Durst—and talk about the contest win. I said absolutely." The next morning, Harmston and Durst met at Acme before riding over to the morning show on 93X, the hard rock station in Minneapolis.

"I was nervous. This was really exciting for me," Harmston

continues. "I had never been on the radio before. So we get there and I'm sweating and not saying much. I'm like, *What do I say? When do I say it?* Meanwhile Will is just throwing out jokes left and right, and I'm just sitting there waiting. Finally they threw me an intro like, 'We're here with the Funniest Person in the Twin Cities contest winner Tim Harmston. Tim, how did it go last night?' And I just kind of go, 'It was so fun. I just did my jokes and then I won.' And they just went, 'OK, so back to you, Will!' I'm sitting there thinking I blew it, and I need to assert myself into the conversation. Show dominance, you know? So they come back from break and they're talking about the Pamela Anderson and Tommy Lee sex tape, and they say, "What do you think about it, Will?" and he's throwing out these great one-liners. Then they ask me, and I say, 'That Tommy Lee has got a *lot* to work with.' And there's this really long pause, followed by the DJ going, 'That's the funniest person in the Twin Cities. Tim Harmston won the Funniest Person Contest last night at Acme.' I just sat there the rest of the time so embarrassed. Like, damn, that was stupid. It was a pretty silent ride back to Acme, where they dropped me off. At that point the elation of the night before had definitely worn off."

Whether it was his radio flub or some X factor he was still missing in Lee's eyes, Harmston didn't get regular time at the Acme open mic for nearly a year following his win. Mack, on the other hand, became one of the fastest-rising stars at the club. "I think Louis promoted me from emcee to feature after, like, three times," Mack laughs. "Louis said to me, 'You no good at hosting. You feature.' Never before in Acme history was there a host who was so bad that they promoted her to feature immediately."

While Mack was doing well for herself at Acme, getting stage time as a female was proving far more complicated outside of the club. "It was so hard for women to get stage time," Mack recalls. "I thanked Mindy for letting me have that stage time. I owed everything to her. At Acme, I featured from about 2003 to 2006, and then I got promoted to headliner."

On the road, however, that success wasn't translating with other comics and club managers who weren't familiar with her track record. "Louis went to bat me for me when people wanted to cancel my bookings because they were afraid to have a female comedian on the lineup," Mack says. "One time I was supposed to open for Darrell Hammond in Georgia, and he wanted to cancel me because he didn't want a woman opening for him. Louis called the club, and he called Darrell's manager. They said they didn't want someone who was political or dirty, and Louis said, 'She'll do a great job for you.' They ended up keeping me, and that show opened so many doors for me. I really wouldn't have the career that I have today if I hadn't started at this club." Eventually, Harmston also broke through and moved his way up the Acme system, making it to headliner status and traveling the country. Both comics carved out successful careers for themselves and, most importantly, started a life together that went beyond the stage.

While Harmston and Mack were able to use the contest as a launching pad to long, prosperous comedy careers, the majority of folks who sign up for the Acme contest are first timers, who see performing stand-up on the club's stage as a bucket list item they can try once and then move on. But occasionally, one of those people finds they have a secret talent for comedy. People like Brooks Robinson. A Stillwater native, Robinson had never been to a live comedy show until he attended one at Acme. "I had a friend who worked there as a doorman, and he got us tickets," Robinson recalled during his time on the FPC podcast. "I saw the contestants that night, and I thought, *I can do better than that*, so I signed up, and the next week was my night."

Despite being a fan of comedy, Robinson had never even considered performing prior to signing up for the contest. "I had never been to a comedy club before," he says. "I thought I was funny, and I watched a lot of comedy as a kid. But it never occurred to me that I could do it. I didn't even know how you got started." To prepare for his night, Robinson—who was still a teenager at the time—rehearsed in the mirror at home, with a hairbrush serving as his microphone and a CD player as his stopwatch. "I just played something on a CD that I knew was three minutes long," he laughs.

Stage choreography is one thing. Good material is another. Robinson zeroed in on taboo humor and went for it. He himself admits his words weren't the most brilliant he'd ever concocted. "It was hack," he says. "Just gross-out, shock, twist humor. I remember a joke about Valleyfair, the Tower of Terror, my grandma, and having sex with her." Despite the lack of good material on that first night, Robinson turned out to be a natural. He absolutely destroyed the competition, and was rewarded with a prize fit for an amateur. "I got shit," he says, without a hint of sarcasm. "I got beer cozies and a hundred dollars to a bar called Turtles in Shakopee. I wasn't even twenty-one, so me and my friends went there and bought onion rings, then sold the other fifty dollars to some random family for twenty bucks."

The rush of winning was a thrill for Robinson, and he was excited about going back to Acme to compete in the next round. But it almost didn't happen. "I won my first night, and then they emailed out the top twenty-five for the semifinals, and my name wasn't on there," he recalls. "So I fucking pulled a Karen and emailed the manager, like, 'Hey, I did pretty good. Can you double-check to see if I qualify?' And I don't know if, like, someone dropped out or there was an accounting error, but they emailed me back and they were like, yeah, you're in."

Deciding that if it wasn't broke, he wasn't going to fix it, Robinson didn't bother hitting up the open mic or anything else that could have better prepared him for the upcoming rounds. Instead, he went in cold to the semis, once again knocking out his competition and making it to the finals.

Robinson admits that his crowd created a bit of a home court advantage. "I had just moved back from Stillwater to the Cities, and they give you twenty free tickets, so I had no problem getting, like, everybody from my high school to come, plus extras. Actually, one of my friends heckled another contestant in the second round. He said, like, 'nice hat' or something, and that got him really flustered. I felt bad about it, but you know, it's a dirty pool."

When the finals rolled around, Robinson, who until that point had never entertained the idea of being told he wouldn't win, started to sweat. "I remember this guy in a wheelchair," he says. "I was worried about him. I was like, *A fucking wheelchair? He has all of those wheelchair jokes!* It was funny too because they had a ramp for him to get onstage, and Chad Daniels was one of the comics that night and just kept making fun of it. He'd be like, 'Is someone skateboarding? Why do we have this?' That guy ended up getting second place, and his prize was a ski trip to Lutsen." Robinson, though, completed the clean sweep of the FPC contest. He was the only contestant in the history of the competition to run the table without having ever tried comedy beforehand. He'd proven his raw talent and used it to coast to victory. The question now was what to do next.

Robinson began showing up to the weekly open mic night at Acme, where he was welcomed by the comedy community, despite his lack of familiarity with the scene. "I didn't know there was a scene," he laughs. "But everyone was really cool." Part of that camaraderie meant spending time with more experienced and successful comics who were willing to offer advice. "I had a joke about driving a bus. Tracey Ashley came up to me and was like, 'No one believes you drive a bus. You got to write jokes that are real.' But for me, everything I had written to that point had worked, so I was scared to try anything new."

Robinson never became fully enamored of the craft of comedy like other past winners, but he developed his raw ability enough to get hired as an emcee at the club. The repetition and uncertainty, though, proved to be more than he was willing to tackle. "I just assumed that comedians were, like, funny on the spot," he says. "I wasn't ready for the repetition of working on jokes and doing the same material. But I'm also a slave to routine. So if I said something even once onstage and it got a laugh, I was locked in. Even if I hated it, I felt like it worked so I couldn't change it." The artistic push and pull of not wanting to sharpen his existing jokes, combined with the fear of failure if he were to take chances creatively, ultimately sent Robinson out of comedy for good. "Part of the reason I quit is that I wasn't funny," he explains bluntly. "If I wouldn't have seen the contest that night I came to a show, I never would have tried in the first place. Like if it had just been a normal show, I wouldn't have thought, *Oh I can do that*. But you get to see people who are bad at it, and it makes you think, like, *Yeah, I can probably be better than them at least*."

In contrast to Robinson's low-stakes, low-pressure attitude about the contest just a few years earlier, Nate Abshire was looking at the FPC as a matter of life and death. Abshire first tried the contest in 2009, after only a few short months in comedy. Still, he recognized just how important the contest was to building a résumé that bookers would take seriously. "I knew it was a big deal already," he explains. "I actually planned to skip the contest in 2009 and do it in 2010, because I wanted to be good by the time I did it." When Abshire half-heartedly entered the contest in 2009, he wasn't disappointed when he didn't capture the title. But the experience motivated him to focus on making an impact in the following year's FPC, so much so that he chose to spend the next year performing without pay, so that he would still be able to qualify as an amateur comedian. "When it comes to winning the contest, the real prize is working at Acme, if that's what your ultimate goal is," he explains. "If you don't really care, then a thousand dollars is dope. And it's a coup because you're beating people who really care. But for me, the real benefit is being able to do sets in front of the club and the management."

By the time the 2010 contest rolled around, Abshire felt like he was a shoo-in to win it all. In fact, it was widely believed in the local comedy community that this would be Abshire's year. "There were betting pools in the local scene about who was going to win," he laughs. "It was that serious. Everyone knew who was in the contest and who was the favorite. The working comics were definitely paying attention."

While Abshire was familiar with the fact that the past several winners had been hired at the club, he knew it wasn't a sure thing. He was pretty confident, though, about where a victory might lead. "Winning doesn't get you hired, but it definitely gets you a look. Heading into the contest in 2010, it was pretty much agreed within the scene that it was my contest to lose." Abshire's prophecy began to come true. He cruised through the first few rounds of the tournament, highlighting just how much he had grown and developed during the unpaid year of preparation. Unfortunately, Abshire hadn't planned on a wild card by the name of Chris Knutson entering that year's contest.

Knutson didn't have a traditional stand-up background like Abshire, but he had spent years performing sketch comedy and improv, which he was able to carry into his stand-up routine. Abshire knew he had competition. "Within a month of starting stand-up Chris was funnier than me," he admits. "The only reason I know that I was the favorite to win the contest originally is because once Chris started, everything shifted. People would be like, 'Nate was going to win. But now it's definitely going to be Chris Knutson.' That was very difficult for me." Abshire and Knutson went head-to-head, along with three other finalists, to decide once and for all who was the funniest person in the Twin Cities that year. But the universe seemed to be working against Abshire.

Comedian Nate Abshire controversially lost the Funniest Person Contest in the mid-2000s, but still went on to become an Acme headliner. *Courtesy Acme Comedy Company*

"Let me start by saying that I think Chris Knutson should have won the contest," Abshire prefaces before explaining what happened that night. "What happened was it was me, Chris, and three other comics who were hobby comics at best. The way they pick the order for when each person performs is with playing cards. You got five cards, everyone picks one, and that's your slot. So when the manager was shuffling the cards, they flashed. I don't think anyone saw it except for me, but now I knew where all of the cards were. I thought it would be awkward to tell the manager that I saw the cards, so I decided

I just wouldn't pick. So everyone else picks their cards, and I immediately know that I have the bullet spot, which is first. At that point I knew I was going to lose. It's virtually impossible to win a contest from the first spot. The problem that night was that it went me, then three people who didn't know what they were doing, and then Knutson. So I set the bar, then they had nine minutes of material that wasn't good, and then Chris came on and crushed. That's how it played out."

Knutson won the contest. But Abshire's year of preparation had consequences beyond a single competition. In fact, losing didn't hurt Abshire's chances of working at Acme. Prior to the contest finale, he had an audition scheduled to become an emcee at the club. He'd already proven himself. The contest was less about professional advancement and more about pride. "I wanted to prove everybody wrong," he says, referring to those who said early on that Knutson would be the eventual victor. "That's what bugged me." What began as a crushing blow to his psyche ultimately turned out to be exactly what Abshire needed. The loss motivated him in ways he believes wouldn't have been possible had his name been called that evening. "If I would have won, I would have been like, *I did it. I'm good enough*. But I lost, so I didn't take a break or stop to revel in my victory," he explains. "For me, not winning was the best thing that could have happened, because I worked my fucking ass off and got good."

Knutson also had a noteworthy future in comedy, before deciding to retire in 2020. But for Abshire, the lessons learned and the lasting impact of the Funniest Person Contest is something he still stands by today, and even passes down to the next generation of would-be contest winners. "The contest is the end of your extreme early game in comedy," he says. "It's like the first move in chess. You know you're going to move your pawn out in front of your king. But what you do after that is when the real game begins." Even the painful lessons are ones Abshire is grateful to have taken away from his experience. "That rejection is something you need to learn," he explains. "Instead of being told by a booker that you're not ready to headline, and then losing your shit via email on a guy who books twenty clubs. It's a good lesson to learn early. It's an important lesson." Ultimately, Abshire explains, it's the losers who keep comedy going. "Comedy is not for winners," he laughs. "If you're a winner, fucking go win. I want to talk about losing. Comedy is for us. It was invented by losers."

After that year, both the curse and the lock fell by the wayside. New names like Ali Sultan and Aidan McCluskey won the contest and became Acme regulars, while others took their thousand-dollar cash prize and disappeared from the stage forever. Regardless of who wins each year's event, however, the contest continues to serve as a launching pad both for local comics ready to take the next step in their careers and for curious dreamers who stumble into a career they never would have considered before. The Funniest Person Contest has been a staple of Acme since the year the club opened its doors. But in the early 2000s, a much larger, glitzier contest took place at Acme, as Hollywood began to notice the caliber of comics who were emerging from the basement in the North Loop.

• CHAPTER 9 •

LAST COMIC STANDING

(AND A WHOLE BUNCH MORE WAITING IN LINE)

By 2003, stand-up comedy was back. Comedy Central had become a television juggernaut, while a new, younger generation of comics had begun their ascent to stardom. The internet made it much easier for entertainers to connect directly with comedy fans, many of whom were discovering the art for the first time. The year prior, *American Idol* became the biggest ratings sensation in America, with undiscovered singers performing for a panel of judges in hopes of being anointed the best new voice in music. With the success of the show, it wasn't long before Hollywood types decided they wanted to attempt to catch lightning in a bottle once again, only this time focusing their energy on comedians.

The result was a show called *Last Comic Standing,* a multiweek competition where the best stand-up comedians from all over the country would go head-to-head, while living together in a house designed to display their offstage personalities, both good and bad. To find talent for the show, producers hit the road and held open casting calls at the best comedy clubs throughout the country. And that meant heading to Acme.

It wasn't the first time the comedy industry took note of the club. In the nineties, producers occasionally reached out to the club's management to host showcases for various one-off television appearances or festivals. "I started getting a little more involved at that point," says Louis Lee. "Once [Nick] Swardson and Frank Caliendo and a few others popped and credited Acme with giving them an opportunity, people started asking more about the club."

From the Aspen Comedy Festival, which was broadcast each year on HBO, to a revamped version of *Star Search*, talent scouts began to look to Lee to provide input as to what comics he felt might be the next big thing to come from Minnesota. True to form, Lee used this opportunity to shine a light on some of Acme's best homegrown up-and-comers. "I would always use people who were featuring here, or starting to headline a little bit here and there," he recalls. "Sometimes I'd include emcees that were ready to move into a feature. Back then, what the industry wanted was someone who could get a sitcom. They would always ask for somebody young. But at that point, nobody young was that funny. The scene hadn't been built back up yet. But I can't tell them that." By the time *Last Comic* came around, however, things had changed. The network was no longer looking for a performer who could be plucked from the stage and molded into an actor. They wanted a great stand-up whom they could cultivate into even better stand-up. They wanted the next Chris Rock, Dane Cook, or Lewis Black. And the comedy scene across the country was finally in a place where the talent matched the demand.

K. P. Anderson, a Twin Cities comic who made his mark locally in the early 1990s at the tail end of the comedy boom, moved out to Los Angeles around 1993 to pursue the next phase of his career. While he had already spent a decade out west before *Last Comic* decided to come through Acme, he says the reputation of Twin Cities comedy, and more specifically, Acme comics, made it an easy choice for the club to serve as a potential talent hotbed for the show. "I think the way *Last Comic* gets to Acme is when Hollywood and LA start to notice Acme is outlasting places like the Comedy Gallery and Knuckleheads," Anderson explains. "I also think it had a little bit to do with people like me and Maria [Bamford] and Jackie [Kashian] and our wave of comedians going out there and having different corners of the industry where we were making an impact. My managers definitely noticed Acme and started talking about it when discussing clubs in the Midwest."

Anderson's managers were also the executive producers for *Last Comic Standing* and had seen firsthand the level of talent Acme had produced. Eager to replicate that success, they reached out to Lee and arranged for one of their talent search events to be held at the club, also asking Lee for his input once again on who deserved a look. "For *Last Comic* they always have a list of who they want to see," Lee recalls. "Then they also had the line. Did they ask me who they should look at? Yes." One of the names Lee provided was Dave Mordal.

After winning the inaugural Funniest Person Contest at Acme years earlier, Mordal had become a favorite at the club, as well as at other rooms in Minnesota and throughout the Midwest. The Elk River native certainly had the chops to move to a larger market several times throughout his career, but he preferred to stay close to home. Despite all of that, Mordal, with his acerbic comedy style and utter apathy for the idea of fame, decided that if Lee was willing to place his reputation on the line to recommend Mordal to producers, he would go through with the audition. Lee recalls, "The producers for that first season called me and said, 'Do you have any comics you would recommend? If you do, I'll make sure they come in and don't have to stand in line.' I pulled Dave aside and said, 'Go to the audition, give them your name, and you'll get in. Just don't tell anyone else about it.' He had other comics who came with him too, but none of them knew he had already been selected to try out."

Mordal, along with some of his comic friends who had auditioned with him that day, were selected to move on to the next round of the competition, which was to be held in Los Angeles. But as the time ticked away and his fellow comics were receiving information about travel and next steps, Mordal heard crickets. "He came to me on Monday and said, 'Everyone else is leaving on Wednesday and I haven't gotten a call,'" Lee remembers. "Around this same time, there was some reality show on Fox where something really bad came out about one of the contestants, and I figured out that's why NBC was holding back on Mordal."

Years before the start of his comedy career, Mordal had been arrested for robbing a gas station in his hometown. While some people would have wanted to bury that memory, Mordal used it as a joke in his act. "It's not a good idea to rob a gas station when you live in a small town," Mordal would say onstage. "The police asked the gas station guy, 'What did the thief look like?' and he said, 'He looked like Dave.'" Lee was convinced this incident was a sticking point that could ultimately keep Mordal from advancing in the reality competition. Though Lee was not typically inclined to involve himself in business outside of Acme, he decided to intervene on Mordal's behalf. "I called the producer and asked if that was the reason why they hadn't called him, and they said yes," Lee says. "I told them, 'He never tried to hide it. You've seen it in his act. And it's a great angle for a TV show.' The guy listened and said, 'Yeah, you're right.' That night after he [Mordal] got done doing the open mic, he got the call telling him to come out."

Mordal made it to California and landed a spot on the show. He became one of the breakout stars of the first season of *Last Comic Standing*. He didn't win the grand prize, but his gruff personality and sarcastic delivery made him the talk of the comedy world, leading to appearances on TV shows like *The Tonight Show* and *Tough Crowd with Colin Quinn*. Mordal's star was burning bright, but it might not have ever happened if Lee hadn't stepped in and made that phone call. "One thing about me is that I know my place," Lee sighs. "I don't pretend to be a kingmaker or act like I'm powerful because I'm not. But when I see something really wrong, like comics getting screwed by the industry, I might say something behind the scenes."

While *Last Comic* launched Mordal's career, his fellow Twin Cities comic Maggie Faris had a much different experience. Like Mordal, she was placed on Lee's short list of local comics who he believed would be a strong fit for the reality competition. Unfortunately, Faris discovered just how unfair the TV business could truly be. "It was hard for me, because that first season when Dave got on, we were with him," Faris recalls. "We waited outside in the subzero temps, we're exhausted, and we have like one or two minutes to charm these executives. And I happened to go right after this mediocrely funny, beautiful woman who they loved. They laughed and said all of these great things, and she got to go through to the next round. Then I got up there and after about ten seconds they're like, 'OK. Thank you.' And I'm thinking, *That's all I get because I'm not a hot lady?* So I opened my mouth and argued with them a little bit. I said, 'You let this hot girl through but not me?' They were stunned. And the next year they let me go through to the next round because I was gutsy and ballsy and said what I believed was right."

K. P. Anderson was brought in at the end of season one of *Last Comic* to serve as a writer for host Jay Mohr. However, once the show became a success and a second season was ordered, he quickly found himself tapped to be a producer. For season two, the show broadcast clips of the tryouts that took place all over the country. Once again, Acme was front and center. "I'm such a hometown guy that defiantly, right or wrong, I'm going to say that Minneapolis holds its own with all the great comedy towns," says Anderson. "For that second season, they actually kept me out of the talent search because of my stand-up roots. They didn't want me hovering around Ross and Bob [the executive producers] because people who knew me would think I was putting my thumb on the scale. But what I was able to do was sit around the table and give names for who I thought should get a look. I remember I was really big on John DeBoer and Michael Thorne. The thing with the show was that not many people actually got selected—or even the chance to try out—from the open casting call. It was all about the preselected talent that we wanted to put in these places. Great comics will rise anywhere, but Acme just kept bringing them."

While the show was an opportunity to showcase some of the very best that Acme had to offer in the comedy world, *Last Comic Standing* was still, at its core, reality television. It still needed its fair share of oddballs, weirdos, and goofs who had no business competing with real comics like Mordal. Most of these folks could be hand selected from the massive cattle call of humanity outside the club. People in costumes, prop comics, and acts that were less funny and more bizarre were brought in to break up the buffet of truly talented performers. While Louis Lee undoubtedly understood this dynamic ahead of time, Anderson says he believes Lee was concerned that the show could accidentally tarnish the reputation he had been building at Acme for more than a decade. "I would guess that Louis was happy for the national recognition of the club, but he was also wary of what the finished product looks like when a reality show comes to town," says Anderson. "He's too smart and too savvy not to know how it worked, and I think he was worried that the business of the club could get out of his hands, and there would be too much shitty comedy showcased on his stage."

Despite any concerns he may have had, Lee says the decision to have talent scouts and shows like *Last Comic* at the club was a good one. Not because of the publicity they brought to the club, but because of the message it sent to the comics. "I'd get really nervous every time there would be an audition or a showcase," he says. "I wanted them [the comics] all to do well. It was never about me. If the producers didn't like any of the comics and wanted to blame me, I didn't care. But it was great because these comics who worked so hard and wanted a chance to be seen by a bigger audience could do it without having to go to LA or New York. I didn't want any of them to move before it was their time. So I looked at it like the more shows that wanted to do showcases at Acme, the better. Local comics will think, *I can stay in Minnesota because I'm still going to be seen by industry people*. That was the real reason I liked having a relationship with LA people and New York people."

After a brief cancellation in 2004, NBC brought *Last Comic Standing* back once again in 2006, with St. Paul native Josh Blue winning the contest. Between Blue and Mordal, the show had begun to serve as a spotlight for the level of talent Minnesota had to offer. In 2007, the producers decided to make Acme a centerpiece for the show, choosing to film the entire audition there (as opposed to only showing snippets as they had done in the past). Sarah Drew (formerly Sarah Remus during her early years at Acme) had become a manager at the club only a year or so prior to filming. While she and her fellow managers were excited about seeing a major TV production unfold before their eyes, Drew says Lee remained characteristically subdued. "NBC came into the club, and their production took over everything," she recalls. "It was exciting for us because we got to see so many big names coming through, and we all got to take pictures sitting in the judges' chairs and stuff like that. But Louis didn't seem overly excited about the whole thing. He just wanted everything to go as smoothly as possible. He said yes to anything they wanted to do, but it seemed like his attitude was sort of, *This is a little bit bullshit, but we're doing it anyway*."

Whether he thought it was bullshit or not, the filming solidified the fact that the industry had come to respect Lee and

Acme as a haven for new comedy talent. "It all trickles down from the club owner," Kathleen Madigan, one of the judges for the season, told the *Star Tribune* before the show's premiere. "He's 20 times smarter about comedy than others."

The auditions were held that March, and a record number of comedy hopefuls slept on the street outside the club, awaiting their chance to be the next Blue or Mordal. Just as in past seasons, however, the majority of the comics who made it in front of the judges had the luxury of sleeping in a real bed the night before, their appearances prearranged. "You got to see how bullshit the open casting call really was," Drew continues. "Like a few crazy people who waited a long time got in, but I felt bad for the real, aspiring comedians who slept overnight and never even got to try out. It's just eye-opening as to how reality TV really works."

One of those aspiring comics was Andy Erikson, who actually made the show in 2015, coming in second overall. But back in 2007, Erikson was just a wide-eyed dreamer who had yet to begin her comedy career and decided to roll the dice and join in the chaos outside the club anyway. "I stood in that cattle call line, and I was, like, number two hundred. I had never even tried comedy before," she laughs. "But I didn't understand how comedy worked at that point. I figured, you go on *Last Comic Standing* and that's how you get to be a comedian." Erikson's mom drove her from their home in Blaine, an outer-ring suburb north of Minneapolis, to the club the night before the auditions, to help her daughter chase her dream of reality TV stardom. After doing a mandatory sweep of the area like any good mom would, she deemed it safe enough for her daughter to come back in the wee hours the following morning.

"I had never even been inside the club before that night," Erikson continues. "But it was just so cool seeing all the comics hanging out. I didn't even go see a show. It was just like this buzz of energy. Then I went home and practiced my set, and the next morning my mom dropped me off at like 4 or 5 A.M., and I stood in line with a bunch of people who thought they were funny." Despite her determination, Erikson didn't get to try out that day. "My mom came that afternoon and picked me up and was just like, 'Well, we'll try again next time.'"

The show continued airing the auditions in the seasons that followed, with Acme being featured each time. After another cancellation in 2010, a revamped version was brought back in 2014. This time, producers reached out to a handful of clubs, inviting them to host preselected showcases featuring some of the area's best talent. Unlike past years, when contestants would parade into the club and perform roughly sixty seconds of material for a mostly empty room early in the morning, these shows happened at night with a full audience having the chance to watch local favorites performing their best stuff for a national viewership.

Robert Baril, an Acme mainstay who had been performing comedy for nearly five years by the time 2014 rolled around, had just been hired by the club a few short weeks prior to the *Last Comic* showcase. While the sense of pride Baril felt from being hired at his home club was overwhelming, he admits he was slightly disappointed that his newbie standing likely meant Lee wouldn't select him as one of the participants. "I hadn't even done a week at Acme yet by that point," Baril recalls. "I was an Acme comic in name only. So when the auditions came together, I figured I didn't really count as an Acme comic just yet, and I'd probably miss that one." While Baril wasn't selected for one of the three-to-five-minute showcase slots that night, he soon found that Lee had a bigger plan for him. "Louis told me that I was going to be emceeing those shows," he says. "He explained to me that I had sort of the sweet spot for the evening, because the producers were going to see me eighteen times or whatever it was, every time I brought up a new comic. I wouldn't get to do a ton of material, but I could throw in a few zingers. It turned out he was right."

Baril was thrilled to be given his first Acme assignment, albeit an unusually chaotic one. "It was really exciting to go from whatever shit gig I had before to doing Acme and being like, 'TV auditions for everyone!'" he laughs. Baril was offered the opportunity to fly to New York for the next round of the competition. "I got to be in front of Wanda Sykes [who had taken over as producer for the show] and some of the other producers at Broadway Comedy Club," he recalls. "Honestly, at that point, it was all gravy to me. I figured I'll ride this out as much as I can, but I looked at it like I had already been hired at Acme, which was the real dream I had been chasing for years."

Despite not making it to the next round of the competition, Baril immediately recognized the respect that came with being anointed an Acme comic. "It was pretty surreal. If you're a comedian in the Twin Cities, getting to Acme is like playing for the Yankees," he recalls. "For Louis to trust me enough to host those auditions and for picking me to represent the club, it gave me the confidence to be like, *Yeah, I can do this*. You don't want to let it go to your head, but now you're not just watching; you're playing for the Yankees." Baril continued to grow and develop at Acme in the months and years that followed, and like many before him, he had already seen the way Lee and the club cared for comics. "Chasing TV credits is cool, but what's much cooler is the loyalty you get from Acme," he continues. "Once you're a part of Acme, you're part of the family. That gave me so many more opportunities than I ever would have had on *Last Comic Standing.*"

By the time the show wrapped its final season in 2015, with a much more polished and prepared Erikson beaming on air about her history with Acme each week until the finale, *Last Comic Standing* had helped share with all of America that the club deserved the same level of respect and admiration as any of its coastal peers. And while industry insiders recognized Lee as the captain who steered the ship, he was still shrouded in mystery to the casual comedy fan, even in his own backyard. Soon, however, his identity became publicly synonymous with the business he had worked to build for the previous two decades, and he was forced to reluctantly receive the praise he rightfully deserved.

• CHAPTER 10 •

TURNING TWENTY

When it came to marking anniversaries, Lee knew how to throw a party. In 1996, Acme celebrated its five-year anniversary with "5 Weeks of Comedy for the New Millennium." Though it may not have been as futuristic as the marketing made it out to be, the month was stacked with headliners including Maria Falzone, Jack Mayberry, and Lee's personal favorite comedian, Dana Gould. When the club celebrated a decade of laughs in 2001, Lee decided to take the party down the street to the Orpheum Theatre in downtown Minneapolis, with a massive show featuring two of the then hottest headliners in the country: Frank Caliendo and Lewis Black. While these shows boasted impressive lineups, the reality was that Acme had carved out a reputation for having the best comedians every week of the year. What other clubs around the country would have looked at as special event shows featuring a once-in-a-lifetime collection of comics was business as usual for Acme.

So when 2011 rolled around, and the club was looking at celebrating its twenty-year anniversary, its staff knew they had to do something even grander. Past anniversaries had featured the biggest names of the moment, but Lee wanted this celebration to be different. He wanted it to reflect the club itself.

He wanted to celebrate with the people who made it into a jewel of North American comedy.

"Louis wanted it to be fair," says Sarah Drew, who was Lee's right hand for what became a milestone event in the club's history. "Any headliner of the last twenty years got an email, just to see who was interested. I remember sending out that email, and just going through that roster was insane. There were so many people who wanted to do it but couldn't fit it into their schedule, and so many really talented people who didn't make the final cut. It was really exciting to see how much love the club had. Louis was really surprised by that. He didn't think there would be a lot of interest." For once, Lee was wrong. The outpouring of interest and love from comics of all generations led him to decide that this anniversary party was too big for just one night. They were going to need a full week.

The Acme Comedy Company twenty-year anniversary party was scheduled for November 1 through 5, with four headliners sharing the bill each night. "It felt like summer camp," continues Drew. "When he was trying to tailor the lineup for each night, he had a really hard time figuring it out." The final lineup included a mix of comics who had gotten their start at the club, like Tracey Ashley and Tim Harmston, breakout comedians who weren't Acme originals but whom the club had helped reach a new level of fame, like Doug Benson and Ryan Stout, and more tenured comics who had been performing at Acme since it first opened its doors in the nineties, like Tim Slagle and C. Willi Myles.

Myles got his start in comedy in the late 1980s in St. Cloud, but his fellow comedians eventually convinced him to move to the Twin Cities. "Louis was very good to me," Myles recalls. "He was the first club owner who gave me a regular headlining gig. He was only going to book me as a headliner, which I appreciated because at that point in my career I really wasn't comfortable going back to featuring or anything like that. He also let me choose my own opener, which was a big deal for me

One of the longest-tenured Acme comics, C. Willi Myles, back onstage at his home club during the twentieth anniversary week. *Courtesy Acme Comedy Company*

because I only wanted to work with people who were going to be clean. I had an audience that didn't want to hear profanity or harsh language, and Louis trusted me enough to pick my own opener that would fit with what I did."

Myles became an Acme regular for years. Along the way, he and Lee developed a close friendship. So when he got the call to be a part of the anniversary, saying yes was a no-brainer. "He called me and said, 'You've always been good to Acme, and we consider you one of our favorites,'" Myles says. "By that time, I really wasn't doing clubs anymore. I only wanted to do corporates and colleges and theaters. But when Louis asked, I immediately agreed to be on the show. Louis was good for comedy, and I wanted to be there for him."

Another comic who was invited to be a part of the festivities was a local legend: John DeBoer. Despite getting his start in Minneapolis a few years prior to Acme opening for business,

DeBoer may well be the first-ever Acme comic who worked his way from emcee to headliner. "I was emceeing at first, but they moved me up to feature pretty quickly because I was featuring in Scott [Hansen]'s clubs," DeBoer recalls. "I was probably one of those guys who headlined way before he was ready at the Comedy Gallery. Through the first half of the nineties, I would emcee and feature at the club. It didn't really matter to me when I went up, just as long as I was working. Then around 1996 or 1997, Louis had a headliner fall out for a night, and he let me . . . try and prove myself. After that, he booked me every year as a headliner. My favorite place in the world is on that Acme stage."

For DeBoer, being invited to participate in the anniversary week was less about bragging rights and more about recon-

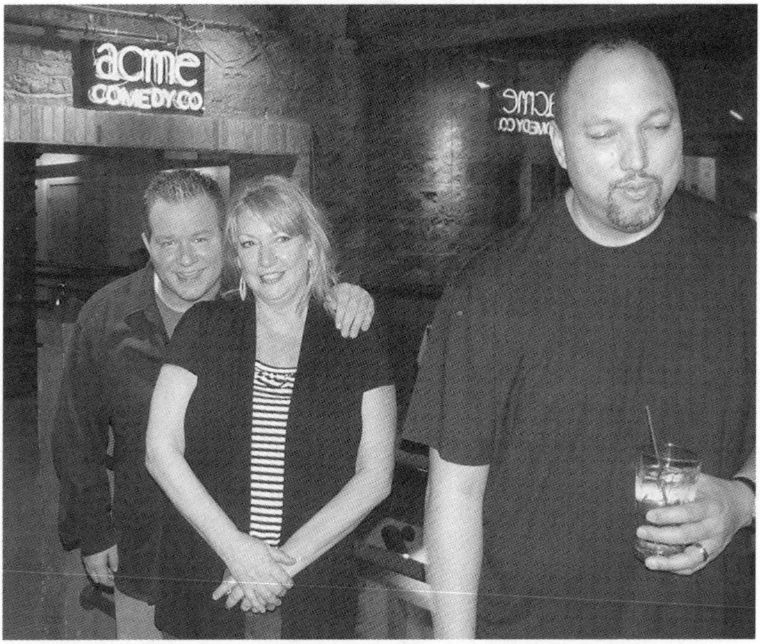

Comedy summer camp during the Acme twenty-year anniversary, including (left to right) John DeBoer, Darlene Westgor, and Kermet Apio. *Courtesy Acme Comedy Company*

necting with people he had grown up with. "It was awesome," he says. "All of these favorites came in from out of town. It wasn't about superstars. It was about the people who made that club and kept it going for so long. Plus you had local people who weren't comics that used to work there that came out too. It was all of your friends you grew up with at the club. It was just really special to be included."

Hosting twenty headline comedians across five shows in three days would demand of anyone a herculean effort. But Lee decided that this week needed *even more*. He booked two showcase nights of up-and-coming local emcees and features as a way to celebrate the future of Acme while creating opportunities for the younger comics to learn from their peers. From Brandi Brown to Cy Amundson, Lee was excited to show off his next generation of comics to the Acme alumni, also hoping to create new opportunities for networking and career advancement.

A late-night conversation with his old buddy Tim Slagle birthed another wild idea for a TV project. Lee decided to make it a reality during the twenty-year anniversary week. "The idea was that every comic has sort of a go-to recipe they cook when they're on the road and stuck in a condo," Slagle explains. "So every week, we would go into the condo and learn how the comics cook. We could pitch it to a hotel chain that had kitchenettes in the rooms, and it would sort of be like, *If you're looking to cook in the room during your stay, here are some funny people to show you how to do it*. But Louis being Louis, he decided he wanted to take it one step further."

In fact, Lee took it several steps further. For the twenty-year anniversary, he filmed three comics—Mary Mack, Chad Daniels, and C. Willi Myles—as they prepared a dish of their choosing. From grocery shopping to providing background about their on-the-road recipe to ultimately cooking the dish in a hotel kitchenette, each comic brought their own unique personality to the experience. They were even invited to cook their dishes live on KARE 11, the local Minneapolis NBC affiliate. After they made their dishes, Lee hired an award-winning chef named Vincent Francoual, who specialized in classic French cooking, to tweak the dishes and, according to a quote from Drew in the local *City Pages*, "make them edible." "*The Comedy Kitchen* is what he was calling it," Myles laughs. "Louis called me and told me this idea, and he knew I could cook. I thought it was a great idea. Something different. Plus it's literally what I do when I'm on the road. I stay at the hotel and I cook."

Lee had always tried to encourage a healthy sense of competition among his comics. So he decided to include all three comic-inspired dishes on Acme's menu for the entire week of the twenty-year anniversary, with 20 percent of the proceeds from each dish going to Fraser, a provider of autism services in Minnesota. Additionally, the comedian whose dish sold the best would be crowned *Comedy Kitchen* champion, and have a donation made to the local charity in their name. While Mary Mack's chicken Asian noodles and Chad Daniels's seasoned pork loin were both delicious, C. Willi Myles's penne pasta with turkey Italian sausage was the biggest hit of the week. "It was a landslide," Myles adds, not playing humble when it comes to his culinary superiority. "It was like three of mine to every one of theirs. Plus I became very good friends with Vincent that week, so it was a great experience all around. I still have my little chef trophy I got from Louis. But there was definitely no money changing hands or anything like that."

Aside from being an opportunity to recognize Acme for reaching the milestone anniversary, the performances audiences were treated to throughout the week were nothing short of incredible. On the first night of the anniversary shows, Chad Daniels, Pete Lee, Tim Harmston, and Mary Mack took the stage, in what quickly turned into a friendly game of one-upmanship. Before the show, the four comics drew cards to determine the order, reminiscent of their time in Acme's Funniest Person Contest many years earlier. The luck of the draw decided that Mack should close the show that night, following Daniels, who was experiencing a massive comedy ascension. After a brief argument backstage, with Mack insisting that trying to follow Chad—who, in Mack's words, "was going to be funny and swear a whole bunch"—would be a tough task for her to tackle despite being a battle-tested headliner, Daniels finally relented and took the last slot of the evening. But if anyone thought he would abandon his take-no-prisoners attitude and soften his approach for the celebration, Daniels quickly buried that notion in his first sixty seconds onstage.

"Please rise as we honor our country with the singing of 'America the Beautiful,'" he said into the mic as he walked onstage. The crowd giggled and shifted in their seats, waiting for the punch line. Daniels didn't back down. "Please rise," he repeated with a straight face. "I'm going to fucking stand up here

Night one of the anniversary week included Acme favorites Tim Harmston, Pete Lee, Mary Mack, and Chad Daniels. *Courtesy Acme Comedy Company*

until you rise," he barked, before taking a seat on a stool. Eventually he launched into song and delivered a surprisingly good rendition of the patriotic classic. It was the first, but certainly wouldn't be the last, memorable performance of the week.

The comics unofficially deemed the second night "Who's your daddy night?" due to the fact that all four comics got their start in the nineties and, as Lee jokingly put it, "If your mom was hanging around the club in the early nineties, there's a chance that one of those comics could be your daddy." Favorites like Slagle, Dave Fulton, Kermet Apio, and David Crowe took the stage, serving as a reminder of the quality Acme was able to deliver, even in the leanest years of stand-up comedy. But the best performance on that night didn't happen onstage; it happened in a back room for an audience that could all fit inside of an elevator.

As the club began to clear out, Slagle appeared in the back, clad in his fez hat, and casually asked the waitstaff, "Hey, can we do a wedding back here real quick?" Before anyone could ask if he was serious, local couple Bob Jakubowski and Theresa Cherney walked in carrying a marriage license. Slagle wasn't kidding. "The day before my show, I posted on Facebook that I was now authorized to perform marriages in the state of Minnesota," Slagle explains. "I was officiating another wedding later in the year, so I needed to get certified, and it just so happened to coincide with the twenty-year anniversary. This couple, Bob and Theresa, were fans of mine and would interact with me on Facebook pretty regularly. They said that they wanted me to marry them, and I told them I would be happy to oblige." It was a brief ceremony, with one of the bride's close friends along with a randomly selected audience member serving as witnesses. Afterward, Jakubowski admitted he had no prior knowledge of his impending nuptials at the club until earlier that day, but he was elated that he and his new bride could have such a special moment in Acme history. After

Slagle signed off on the paperwork, it was time to get back to the party. And what a party it was.

In comedy, when someone reaches headliner status, they typically find themselves more isolated and less connected to the friends they made in their early comedy days. "Everyone is on the road, and you aren't touring around with your peers because they're headlining and traveling too," explains Harmston. "So when the lineup came out for the week, I couldn't believe I got to see so many people I hadn't seen in so long. I remember thinking, *Enjoy this. This might be one of the most fun weeks you'll ever have*. And it was."

Myles was another comic who was excited to catch up with some of the names from his past, even if they wouldn't all remember their conversation the next day. "The problem was that Louis had everything for free," laughs Myles. "I excused myself quite early in the night, but there were a lot of stories being told and a lot of lies being told. A lot of people misremembered a lot of things and took some liberties with things that did not happen. There were some comics, I won't mention any names, who considered themselves geniuses who were not geniuses. I had to explain to them that they were getting carried away with that label. But honestly, it was a lot of fun and really interesting to see where everyone was at in their lives."

Clear or clouded, the memories flowed almost as freely as the booze during the week, which Drew remembers as having possibly the craziest after-parties in club history. "It was wild," she laughs. "On Friday night, I remember telling all of the comics, the headliners and the emcees, that we were going to take this picture for Louis of all the comics at the club on Saturday. I walked in that morning, and apparently people had just left the bar an hour earlier. The place was trashed, there was no alcohol left. Everyone showed up late, completely hungover, asking for Bloody Marys, and I was like, 'Fuck you. I'm dying right now. Get your own drink.' Those after-bars were so fun. The after-bar at Acme is always fun, but we went until daylight for several days. I was in rough shape at the end of it, but man it was fun."

Saturday was the grand finale shows of the weekend, featuring comics like Dwight Slade, Jackie Kashian, and John DeBoer, among others. After the final show, all the comics and staff headed to the event center next door for a closing party, which got plenty raucous, but also occasioned a walk down memory lane, featuring multiple generations of Acme comics. "It was awesome," says DeBoer. "It wasn't about superstars. It was about the people who made that club for so long. Plus with all of the local people who were there, it was like having all of your friends you grew up with in one place. We played a game that last night at the after-party, where everyone was doing Dwight York bits. It was a contest where somebody would do a setup and someone else would have to do the punch line. It went on for a fucking hour straight. It was a testament to Dwight that all of these different comics knew that much of his material. It was a lot of fun to watch. Then we did it with someone else, and then they did it with my act. That part of the game was really short."

As a token of his appreciation, DeBoer created a poster of Lee that was reminiscent of the movie poster for *The Godfather*. While it made for a fun visual, DeBoer says the analogy was fitting. "I would always call him Don Louie because he was like our godfather," he explains. "But he was a good godfather. He won't kill you; he just won't book you anymore. Personally, I'd rather be killed. Then at least I'd have an excuse." But for all of the comedy, debauchery, and celebration, the most interesting part of the twenty-year anniversary week had to be watching Lee. Not only was he able to enjoy the fruits of his tireless labor from basically the moment he arrived in America, but he was also able to share his story of struggle, perseverance, and triumph publicly for the very first time.

Everyone from the *Star Tribune* to alt-weekly institution *City Pages* to the *St. Paul Pioneer Press* ran front-page stories about Acme's incredible achievement and the man who made it all possible. "I was so proud of how much press we had for the week," beams Drew. "It felt like every time you turned on the TV or listened to morning radio or opened a newspaper, they were talking about Acme."

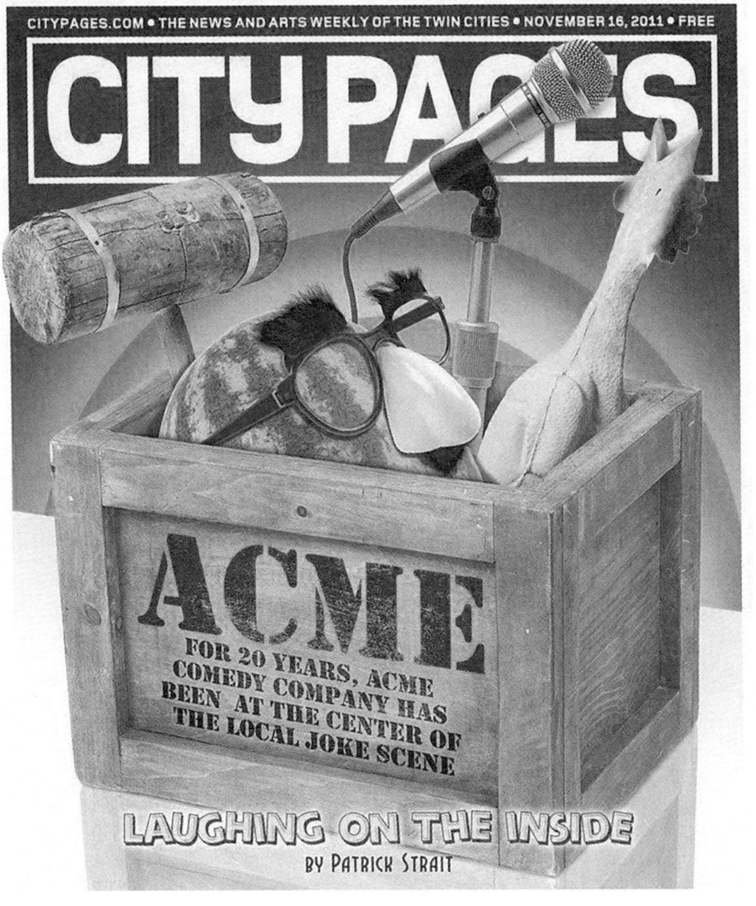

City Pages was one of numerous media outlets that covered the milestone anniversary. *Courtesy Patrick Strait*

A lot of jokes, a lot of laughs, and a lot of memories in one room, as (nearly) every comic who performed during the week toasts Acme's history. *Courtesy Acme Comedy Company*

While the celebration was a massive success by all measures, the reality was that Lee still carried some pretty serious baggage. He was still carrying the weight of his teenage self who struggled with low expectations. Still carrying the shame of a son who had put his family in financial peril. And still carrying the feeling that there was unfinished business in his homeland that he had left decades earlier. But if there was one thing Lee had proven to that point, it's that he wasn't one to give up. And after the success of the twenty-year anniversary, there had never been a better time to prove that sometimes, you can go home again.

• CHAPTER 11 •

HOME TO HONG KONG

When Louis Lee left Hong Kong with his siblings in the 1970s, he was dejected, insecure, and looked upon as the black sheep of his family. In the decades that followed, he had proven his worth to his family and, more importantly, to himself. When he traveled back home to Hong Kong to visit with family and friends, he always kept his professional accomplishments in the United States to himself. "Your profession is very much looked at as a reflection of who you are," Lee says of Chinese culture. "What you do is who you are. The people at home didn't understand what I do. If you grew up in Hong Kong, they don't have the same kinds of comedy clubs like they did in America."

But by the early 2000s, stand-up comedy had begun to reach a more global audience. While some countries were still in the early phases of finding their comedy voice and establishing a scene of their own, a promoter in Hong Kong named Jami Gong was thinking bigger. Gong, a Chinese American who was born and raised in New York, had a lot in common with Lee. He was one of six children, was raised by hardworking parents, and fell in love with comedy at an early age. Though Gong was a comic himself who performed shows throughout the Chinatown district of New York City, he began promoting shows and found he had a desire to bring stand-up to an untapped Chinese audience. After making several trips back and forth from New York to Hong Kong, Gong finally decided to take a risk and open TakeOut Comedy Club Hong Kong, which was the first full-time comedy club in Asia. "My hope in the beginning was to find the next Chinese Chris Rock or Jerry Seinfeld," says Gong.

During a visit to his homeland, Lee decided to stop at Gong's club to see how things were progressing. "The comedy world of Hong Kong kind of knew me because Americans would come to perform and they knew about Acme," Lee explains. "Plus Jami grew up in New York, so he knew who I was. I decided to go to the club and see what he was doing. I watched the showcase, and I could tell what level they were at. It was like the eighties all over again. A bunch of people doing comedy in a bar trying to get discovered."

Despite being at two different places in their careers, Lee and Gong developed a relationship, with Lee taking an interest in nurturing Gong the way he had comedians back in America. "At that point we were probably the only two Chinese comedy club owners in the world," laughs Lee. The best way Lee could think to mentor Gong was simple: he needed to show Gong how he promoted comedy, and what stand-up could look like in China. But to do that, he needed to return home. "Jami came to me and said, 'Why don't you put together a show and bring it here?' " With that, Lee began plotting what would be the first-ever Acme Comedy tour throughout Asia. "I wanted to bring in three pros who were well established, so that the comics and audience could see the difference," Lee explains. "My point was that I wasn't trying to control this group. I wanted to introduce my group and show Jami how I did things. Then he can decide if it's what he wants to do. That was the whole spirit."

The tour would take place in August 2014, and would make three stops: Hong Kong, Singapore, and Macau. The first thing Lee needed to do was decide who was going to perform during the tour. It would be his first time traveling with a group of comics for a full week, and whoever he brought along would be representing not only Acme but also Lee himself. He needed comics who he knew would put on the best possible show, while also demonstrating respect for his homeland.

His first two choices were easy picks: Pete Lee and Chad Daniels. Aside from the fact that both comics had gotten their start at Acme, they also had two very different styles of comedy, which Lee was interested in bringing together. "Pete is a very friendly comic," says Lee. "Chad, at the time, was a very bitter comic. They both had strong personalities, and to build the show, I wanted two of the very strongest performers I knew from two different ends of the spectrum." At that point in their careers, both Pete and Chad had become bona fide headliners who had logged thousands of miles traveling all over the world to perform comedy. Despite their experience, however, both were immediately excited, nervous, and overwhelmed at the opportunity that was being presented. "I felt blown away," says Pete. "He called me on the phone and said, 'How would you like to do comedy in Hong Kong and different parts of Asia?' I had just done *Letterman,* and now I'm going to Asia to do comedy? I'm thinking, *What is my life?*"

As for the third member of the crew, Lee initially wanted to bring in Jake Johannsen. Johannsen got his start back in the mid-eighties and was actually a California-based comic who had endeared himself to Lee and become an Acme regular, despite not being a homegrown talent. "Chad and Pete were so opposite of each other, and I wanted someone really seasoned who I could put in the middle," Lee explains. "I wanted someone from the eighties because I thought it would provide a really interesting spectrum of comedy." Unfortunately, scheduling conflicts made it impossible for Johannsen to make the trip. In his place, Lee decided to recruit a fast-rising comic named Tom Segura.

A Midwest comic himself, Segura started his career around

(Left to right) Louis Lee, Pete Lee, Chad Daniels, and Tom Segura pose together in Hong Kong at the start of the Acme Comedy Asia Tour. *Courtesy Sarah Drew*

the same time as Pete and Chad in the early 2000s. Even though Segura was younger than the other two comics, Lee decided that he had the intelligence and polish to complete the trifecta, and asked if he would come along on the tour. "My manager called me and said, 'Louis Lee is putting together this tour of Asia. You weren't the first choice, but the other guy dropped out so he wants to know if you would be interested.' I'm not sure why he needed to tell me that part," Segura jokes. "Just give me the offer. But I said yes, I would love to go."

In addition to the three comics, Lee also decided to reach out to his old friend J. Elvis Weinstein. Besides a successful career as a comedian, writer, and actor, Weinstein had recently directed his first documentary project, about actor and musician Michael Des Barres, and Lee wanted him to take the reins of a film chronicling the trip as his next project. "Louis called me up and said, 'I'm planning this trip, I want to make a documentary about it: do you want to direct it?'" Weinstein recalls.

"At that point his plan was to find investors who would back the project, but he changed his mind and told me he was going to put up the money himself because he didn't want anyone else telling me what to do. So that was our deal. He'd put up the money, I'd put up the labor, and we'd make a movie." That movie would eventually be titled *I Need You to Kill* and would provide an in-depth look at the comedy culture of China, the connection the comics make with one another on tour, and Lee's reflections on returning home.

Rounding out the Acme contingent was club manager Sarah Drew, who was brought in to serve as the tour manager and public relations liaison for the trip. "The other manager at the time had gotten to go with Louis to festivals in Chicago and Montreal, and I was feeling kind of jealous that I wasn't a part of those trips," Drew explains. "When I heard about the Hong Kong trip I was like, 'I am going to be the most annoying motherfucker about this. You need me because of this and that.' I just kept pushing him until he finally agreed. Then I screamed for like five minutes in the office afterwards."

The group convened in Hong Kong that August, and from the very first day, the emotions of each person were very heightened. "I didn't even think about how scary it would be to go do comedy in a whole other hemisphere," says Pete. "I was just excited to be doing something new and crazy with my career." Daniels and Segura echoed Pete's concerns about whether their comedy would translate to Chinese culture and connect with audience members. "I had so much anxiety about starting the week off," Segura said in the documentary. "I really didn't know what to expect," added Daniels. "I wasn't sure if there were going to be huge cultural or language differences or anything like that." Just as Lee had done throughout his career at Acme, however, Louis encouraged all three of the comics to be true to themselves when they got onstage. "He told me, 'I want you to be yourself,'" remembers Daniels. "I don't want you to pull back at all. If you don't like the crowds,

I want you to let them know you don't like them, just like you do in America. This isn't about representing me over there. I want them to get the real you.' I was like, that seems incredibly dumb, but OK."

While the comics spent their days exploring Chinese culture, Lee hit the press circuit. It was a stark contrast to what he was used to doing back in America, where the comics themselves would be at the forefront of print, TV, and radio interviews, and Lee could remain in the shadows, making sure things were running smoothly. But in Hong Kong, Lee was the star. His story of traveling to America and conquering the world of stand-up comedy, only to return home with the hope of imparting his knowledge to the budding Chinese comedy scene was unique, and the Chinese media was eager to learn more.

"He himself had a lot of press," Drew recalls. "Not even about the shows; just himself. I took him to radio interviews, newspaper interviews. It was so great because there was a picture of Louis in the newspaper in Hong Kong wearing shorts.

演藝故事

笑聲傳奇

「棟篤笑」一詞，由黃子華所創，源自西方的「Stand Up Comedy」。每隔數年，香港人才等到黃子華、林海峰等開騷，開懷笑一餐。但在美國，打工仔下班後上酒吧，邊呷啤酒邊看棟篤笑，輕鬆笑一笑。棟篤笑的精粹，在於融入本土文化，所以香港人的棟篤笑，只有香港人才聽得懂，只有香港人才識得笑。生於獅子山下的李啟斌(Louis Lee)剛巧相反，他由一個不諳英語的小男孩，移居美國打滾數十載，最終成為明尼蘇達州棟篤笑界最具影響力的人。 記者 [illegible]

香港小子

炮製美式棟篤笑

成功融入地道文化

開設俱樂部 廚房侍應一腳踢

想為港人演Good Show

While Louis Lee typically preferred to stay behind the scenes, he was the star attraction for Chinese media throughout the Acme Comedy Asia Tour. *Courtesy Sarah Drew*

Apparently he thought it was a good idea to wear shorts the day they were doing photos. The nice thing was that Louis's sister still lives in Hong Kong, where she runs one of the top charitable agencies. She had the scoop on who to call and where to go. Then Neal Justin [a longtime comedy writer for the *Star Tribune*] had contacts in Singapore that he hooked me up with too."

Finally, it came time to perform. The night before the first show, Jami Gong chatted with the comics to give them what can only be described as a pep talk warning. "If Louis Lee brings you over here, I know you're good," Gong says to the comics in the documentary. "This isn't going to be an ordinary road trip. The people you're going to be performing for are very well off and have a lot of connections. That's why the one thing I need from you is I need you to kill."

Despite not being onstage himself, Lee admits he was experiencing preshow jitters of his own. "I was nervous," Lee recalls. "I didn't tell them, but I was. All three of them were excited to be there, but deep down I'm thinking, *You still have to do these shows*. Of course I can't say that, but that's how I felt. It was kind of like the early 2000s all over again. A scout would come to town, I'd put together a showcase, and I'd feel nervous because they represented the scene in Minnesota. So when we went to Hong Kong, I wanted to be proud of them [the comics]. I was anxious for them and proud of them, as opposed to 'look at what I built.'"

With the added pressure from Gong and the high expectations from Lee, the first shows were something of a mixed bag. "That first night onstage I felt like a fish out of water," says Pete. "I'm jet-lagged; I don't know how people are going to receive me; I wasn't sure how my brain was going to react onstage. Fortunately, Asian culture is very kind and respectful. My Minnesota and Wisconsin sensibilities spoke to them. I really wasn't sure how much would connect with them, since

I grew up in the Midwest, but kindness is very important to them. I was very surprised and happy about how my comedic sensibilities played. I was really ecstatic."

While Pete felt comfortable rather quickly, Segura took a little longer to get in a groove. "Singapore felt like a less-developed scene to me," he said in the documentary. "I felt like we were jumping on an open mic. But the open micers were slaughtering." That night, Segura was heckled by an audience member while doing a bit about uncontrollable bowel movements: the man yelled out that he himself had incontinence issues that were brought on by Segura's bad comedy. "I just froze and didn't know what I could come back with," Segura admitted while talking with Pete and Daniels later that night. "I didn't like that first set."

While Segura and Pete were focused on winning over the crowds early on, Daniels felt it was his responsibility to give the audience an authentic experience. "For me it was a respect thing," he shares. "Louis is from here, and he chose to bring us to his home. That means a lot more there than it does in Western civilization. So part of respecting him, to me, was doing what he told me to do. That first night I remember everyone looking at me like, *What the fuck, dude?* because I did an abortion bit in China. And when the audience started groaning about it, I just said, 'Would it make it easier if I said it was the daughter who died?' Louis told me to do that. He told me to be authentic onstage."

The Acme comics weren't the only ones who were trying to maintain their authenticity onstage. The local talent who were working on carving out their own paths in their native countries were still rough given the lack of stage time available as well as the fact that stand-up comedy hadn't quite penetrated the culture to the same degree as it had in other parts of the world, but they were using their platform to find their voices and speak to things that felt important. "[Stand-up comedy] was a dream I never dared to dream," said Rishi Budhrani, a comedian in Singapore who was featured in the documentary. "If you're funny in Singapore growing up, no one encourages you to pursue that. No one talks about it like it could be a career." Despite Singapore's strict rules and regulations, Budhrani and others weren't afraid to take the government to task onstage. "Singapore has one of the best zoos in the world," Budhrani began in one of his jokes. "How is that possible? We don't have any wildlife. There aren't any jungles. Then I realized: the reason we have one of the best zoos in the world is that our government specializes in exerting control over living things in captivity." According to Budhrani, up until that point, stand-up had somehow managed to sneak under the radar of the Media Development Authority, which kept a close eye on theater performances and stage shows. At least, he was pretty sure that was the case. "I get a feeling a bunch of us comedians might already be on their radar," he said. "They might have a folder on us somewhere."

Another comic, Tamby Chan, offered up a bold and unflinching joke about the Tiananmen Square massacre that took place in the late 1980s, when authorities killed numerous students who were protesting for economic reform and social change in China. "I visited Tiananmen Square while I was in China," Chan began. "They have a tagline there just like there are for other tragedies. Like for 9/11 they say, 'Never Forget.' For the Holocaust it's, 'Never Again.' But for Tiananmen Square it's, 'Never Happened.'" Weinstein left the joke in his film, though he later admitted he had regrets about that decision. "Given what would happen after we left, with the protests in central Hong Kong, I felt bad for leaving it in," he says.

Beyond the comedy and business aspects of the trip, Lee was also focused on providing his guests with a true look at his homeland and his personal life that they hadn't seen before. "He was such a gracious host," remembers Drew. "It felt like the trip wasn't just about comedy for him. It was about showing us where he's from. We'd go out for dim sum just for the heck of it. He brought us to hang out with his family just to be nice. It was a different side of him and a different vibe than I had ever seen before." Seeing that side of Lee touched the comics deeply, bringing some of them to tears. "Louis's approval in general means everything to me," says Pete. "He's a kind man but also very discerning. It meant so much that he was willing to bring me in and let me be a part of this. We went to dinner with his family, his mom, and we met everybody. It was a big homecoming. I've said it before that Louis is like a second father to me, and I mean that. This trip was like that moment in *Field of Dreams* where the dad asks his son if he wants to have a catch."

Despite Lee's tendency to downplay the importance of the trip for himself personally, his guests could see how the tour was something of a victory lap and a milestone moment in his life. "It felt like this was his way of saying, 'I'm not the black sheep of the family anymore,'" says Drew. "'I made it, and I'm bringing what I've worked for all of these years to Hong Kong, so that I can show you that the investment you made in me was worth it.' I think it all helped validate his stance in his family." "I saw a couple of different Louises there," Weinstein adds. "I saw a proud papa to his boys. I saw excitement about potentially getting something going comedy-wise in Hong Kong. And I saw a little brother looking up to his older sister, who is this wealthy, important person in Hong Kong." In fact, Lee's sister and her husband attended the final night of the tour, which was much more of a high-end presentation than the previous shows. "My sister loved Chad, and her husband loved Pete Lee," Lee beams. "That was exactly what I wanted."

Lee left Hong Kong on a high, looking forward to the opportunity to bring more comedy to Asia, and to make an impact there like he had done back in Minneapolis. Unfortunately, the world had other plans. "The whole thing collapsed," Lee sighs while reflecting on the events that followed the trip. By 2016, with China experiencing a severe economic downturn, regulators, censors, and government officials increased censorship in an effort to project a stronger image of positive energy across the country. As a result, commentators (or stand-up comedians) were warned that any remarks or projections that were contrary to the official statements would not be tolerated.

"It's a time capsule now," reflects Weinstein. "The protests in Hong Kong totally changed my opinion. You would never be able to get away with making this film today." While clubs like TakeOut Comedy in Hong Kong and Comedy Masala in Singapore are still presenting stand-up, the government involvement has significantly changed what can be said onstage, which is something Lee has always said he would never tolerate in his clubs. "The last thing I would ever do is tell a comic what to say," Lee says plainly. "So when that became an issue, I said, 'I'm out.'"

While Lee may not have had the opportunity to capitalize on the success of the Acme Comedy Asia Tour, Weinstein says the profound impact Lee left on the comics during the trip closed the loop on a full-circle moment of his own journey. "Comedy taught Louis about America," he says. "And then he taught comedy and a bunch of comics about China."

· CHAPTER 12 ·

ACME vs. THE CITY

Louis Lee isn't much for confrontation. From the first few months he lived in America, he recognized right away that some people were going to be rude, inconsiderate, and generally difficult to deal with. But he also knew it wasn't personal. "When I first came here, I would get all kinds of comments, especially working in restaurants," Lee recalls. "When I was in college, people didn't see Asians in Minneapolis. So when someone would say something, I knew not to take it personally. I'm still well trained not to take things personally." But when push comes to shove and his back is against the wall, Lee isn't afraid to fight back.

In 2016, just a few months before the club would celebrate twenty-five years in its existing space in the North Loop, word got out that the City of Minneapolis had sold the parking lot across from Acme; a developer intended to demolish the lot and put up a new condo building in its place. Developer Curt Gunsbury and his Solhem Companies already owned the condo building located around the corner from Acme. His plan was to build an eight-story apartment building that would be located on top of what happened to be one of the main city-owned parking lots that was regularly filled with Acme customers on any given night of the week.

While property redevelopment is a reality of urban planning in any major city, this project didn't sit well with Lee, and he decided to vent his frustrations to the local media. "One of the residents upstairs in our building told me that they were going to build condos in that space," Lee says. "Some private developer who had a few condos in the area. Like I said, I know my place. You don't argue with the big guy. But I decided to talk to *City Pages* and tell them how badly that would screw up parking for us and cause a lot of other problems too."

The article was published in late May, just weeks before the developer intended to break ground. It said in no uncertain terms that the elimination of 130 parking spots from the area would effectively force Acme to close its doors and relocate. "I love the substantial growth that I have seen in the North Loop and welcome new neighbors openly, but the bottom line is that this proposed apartment complex will drive my customers away," Lee explained plainly in the article. "The people who want to see shows at Acme Comedy Company will no longer come here because the parking situation will be a nightmare." Needless to say, Lee's directness didn't sit well with the developer—or the city itself. "The landlord called me and yelled at me on the phone," Lee says with a shrug. "I told him, look, I'm the one who pays rent here. I bring in a thousand people a weekend, which is around two hundred or three hundred cars. [If this building goes up] I'm going to lose $100,000 a year in sales."

In an attempt to quell some of the negativity the story stirred up, Gunsbury himself reached out to *City Pages* to offer his side of the story. He explained that there were still three large parking lots near Acme that were not owned by his company. And in response to the claims that the development would hinder parking for customers, he pointed out that the new apartments would include more than two hundred parking stalls, and that residents wouldn't be using any of the lot space nearby. "At no time has anyone from Acme reached out to us to discuss their parking," Gunsbury said. "We love the place; we want it to stay there. We're very excited because they're a great business. I guess I'm just confused how this blew up so fast."

Whether the statement was true or a bloated PR piece to quell the complaints of those who had reached a boiling point with the perceived overbuilding in Minneapolis at that time, only Gunsbury knows for sure. But for Lee, the demeanor he saw behind the scenes was much different from what was conveyed in the papers. "The reason I spoke up so loudly was because of the attitudes," he explains. "Nobody cared. The city? They don't care. The big developer? They don't care. They all say, 'You're so important to the neighborhood.' I say bullshit."

While Lee himself was furious, he knew his feelings would be tame in comparison to what would happen when the comics got involved. "I told the landlord that once the comics get angry, I have no control over what happens next," Lee recalls. Lee's premonition was spot-on, and the Twin Cities comedy community, as well as the comedy scene across the country, was not ready to sit idly by while one of the most important comedy clubs in the country was muscled out of its home. Longtime Acme comic and comedy superstar Marc Maron tweeted a simple "SAVE ACME!" message. Other comics began reaching out to the building landlord, while some called city officials directly. "The comics were all over them," Lee recalls. "And they thought I was the one who stirred up everything."

Lee may not have directly incited the Acme faithful to mobilize and share their collective issues with the decision, but his anger and sense of concern was palpable to all of those around him. "At first I was just sort of like, *Oh, this is what happens. Things get gentrified,*" explains Sarah Drew. "But Louis was so passionate, and after a little bit it became reality that people really might not be coming to the club anymore. I think we were worked up over the club, but honestly we were worked up over the bigger picture. People were fed up with the city in general and a lot of the decisions that were being made, along with the overbuilding and ugliness of it. It wasn't just about this one condo and this one parking lot."

In response to the news, Acme launched an online petition rejecting the development proposal. They also invited "concerned citizens to attend the City Planning Public Hearing on June 27 at 4:30 P.M., and voice their support for the club." They might as well have hung a curtain and offered drink service, because the meeting became a comics summit. Roughly fifty comedians, ranging from new open micers all the way up to Los Angeles–based David Huntsberger (who happened to be performing at the club that week), showed up to lend their support. "The rest of the world is jealous that Prince lived here. They're also jealous that Acme is here," Huntsberger testified in front of the council, attempting to pull at their sense of local pride. "Don't lose both of them."

Andy Erikson, who was also living in California at the time the news broke, flew back to Minnesota just to be a part of the meeting. "Everyone was talking about it across the country," Erikson says. "You'd go to clubs and people would be like, 'What's happening? Is Acme really closing?' People were doing campaigns to raise awareness. It was like, we can't lose Acme." Erikson, whose mother had served on the city council in her native Ham Lake, had been around the civic process long enough to realize that the odds were stacked against her home club. "I knew there wasn't due process for both sides," she explains. "Like they didn't give enough of a warning for what needed to be done." Erikson was one of many comics who read prepared statements during the meeting, providing an impassioned plea to city officials. But not everyone had the benefit of Erikson's civic experience. "I got up and spoke. I sounded like an idiot," Drew laughs. "Everyone was giving their two cents. That's just the community that Acme breeds. We're a unit. I thought it was really nice to see that collective voice and the whole comedy community coming together like that."

Despite these words of support, the meeting wasn't going Acme's way. Erikson recognized this, which is when her true feelings came out. "The council had a goal, and it wasn't to listen to the people," she says. "It was to get that condo built. I was so upset with the system of power not listening to artists and not listening to the reasons that people even care about going downtown in the first place. I remember staring at these smug city council guys. We're all crying, and they did not care. They just stared at us like, *Your compassion is boring to us*. Finally I stood up and yelled out, 'Come on! Listen to us!' They actually told me to sit down, and I was like, what are you going to do? Arrest me? Their job was to listen and they were laughing at us. So for once, I got to heckle someone. That part was fun. It was some really good stage time." Comic James Moore summed up the comedy contingent's feelings in the meeting nicely. "It would destroy the currently thriving community to not have parking available for residents coming in to support the businesses," he said in his prepared statement.

Though the emotionally charged testimonies shined a massive spotlight on the potential blowback the building project could have from the local arts scene, the council remained steadfast in its view. Members voted to approve the development, though they offered a flimsy compromise that included language requiring the developer to work with local businesses to find a solution to the parking demand. "I'm hoping that the loss of a surface parking lot is not the death of such an outstanding comedy club," said planning commissioner Alissa Luepke Pier. "I hope it's larger than that."

Lee wasn't having it. Following the decision, Lee told the *Star Tribune* that he would start the process of looking for a new property for Acme, and that he was very open to the idea of relocation. "I will start to listen to all kinds of offers," he told the paper. "Let people call." The next several months were extremely uncomfortable for Lee, as well as for the comics who had called Acme home for more than two decades. "It was a weird time, because we were all just waiting to see what happened next," reflects Erikson. "The biggest thing I think we all learned was that the process of how people interacted and communicated with artists was broken. I still don't understand people who get into power, just caring about money and nothing else."

In a last-ditch effort to put public pressure back on the city and the developers, Lee looked to an old acquaintance who just happened to be the biggest comedian in the entire world at the time. "Nick Di Palo was performing at the club, and he's friends with Louis C. K. I asked him if Louis had heard about what was happening," Lee explains. "At that time, he was at the top of his career. I was honest with the comic, and I told him, 'Hey, I really need help. If you talk to him, let him know I could use his support.' He told me that Louis had heard about it, but at that point he wasn't using social media anymore, so he didn't really have a platform to talk about it."

But C. K. would do Lee one better. That August, the longtime Acme comic performed to a sold-out arena audience at the Target Center, just a few blocks away from the club. The morning of the show, C. K. announced a surprise late-night show at Acme that would take place following that night's performance, with all the proceeds going to help Acme as it prepared for the next chapter. "He knew that if he did a show in a club, which at that point you would never see him in a small club anymore, it would get press," Lee recalls.

But all the charity benefits, public grievances, and celebrity endorsements couldn't stop the inevitable from happening. The condo building was built, and Lee began to finalize plans to move to a new location outside of Minneapolis. "I was close," Lee says plainly. "I was near the end of my lease, and I had banks that had already given me letters of intent to make purchases." Drew seconds the idea that Lee wasn't bluffing. "Was he going to leave? Yes. He was really close," she says. "I remember even seeing plans, because he was going to build it brand-new so that it could fit the exact specifications that he wanted." But along the way, Lee had a change of heart. Despite losing his battle with the city, and a whole bunch of parking spots along with it, Lee decided to remain in his existing space. His logic boiled down to the same two factors that ultimately determine success in every aspect of comedy: money and luck.

"The reasons I didn't move were, first, it would have been a huge capital investment," Lee explains, conjuring up ghosts of the financial peril he experienced years earlier. "And the second is superstition. My sister in Hong Kong knows a really good fortune teller. She goes to him all the time to ask about things. When something big is going to happen, she goes to him. So my lease was going to be up in 2018 or 2019, and I was ready to go. I would have to give the landlord one year notice, so I would have given notice probably in 2017. She went to her fortune teller and then called me. She says, 'He said hold tight. Don't move.' I told her that I had gone this far and I wasn't going to back down. So I sat down with my landlord and said, 'You know what? Here's the letter of intent from the bank. And here's the new location where I'm moving to. You have twenty-four hours to work out a better deal for me with your boss or I'm leaving.' He came back the next day, and it was done. He got us a better deal."

While a rational person would have chalked up the decision to sound business sense and savvy negotiation tactics, Lee believes the fortune teller knew what was coming in the future, and that it would be extremely volatile. "The fortune teller was right," he says. "By the time we were ready to move into a new space, it would have been 2020, right when COVID hit. I would have put in a million dollars of my own money, plus I'd owe the bank $1.5 million. And with COVID? We would have never made it through." With live events on a pandemic hiatus, parking would have been the least of Lee's problems. But better terms on a new lease and a renewed sense of the club's importance to the community would prove essential for enduring the pandemic.

Despite the turmoil the club experienced throughout the year it took on the city, the silver lining was that Lee was able to see firsthand just how important Acme, and Lee himself, had become to comedy everywhere. The support he received from the comics showed that they were willing to stand by him even in dire circumstances. But it wasn't long before one of Lee's biggest allies throughout the entire ordeal looked to Lee to return the favor and support the comic during the most difficult phase of his own career.

• CHAPTER 13 •

CANCELED

In 2015, Louis C. K. was the biggest comedian in the world. He signed a massive deal with the cable network FX that included a new prime-time stand-up special, along with multiple television series that he cocreated and produced. He was a box office success, scoring major roles in everything from animated films to dramatic biopics. He was nominated for Emmys, Grammys, and a plethora of other awards. No one else in stand-up in the modern era at that time could compare to what C. K. had accomplished.

So when he went on *The Tonight Show Starring Jimmy Fallon* that spring, gushing about the impact Acme Comedy Company and Louis Lee had on his career to that point, it was like being anointed by comedy royalty. "I remember the first night I got real money," C. K. told Fallon. "I worked at a place in Minneapolis called the Acme Comedy Club, run by a guy named Louis Lee, and it was a club I worked at a lot and it would only be like half full. And you pour your heart into these shows, and they give you like eight hundred dollars, maybe a thousand dollars, and you go on to the next place. It's a sad life." That was until, C. K. explained, he finally packed the place for a full week of shows. "And I had never really done that before. And at the end of the week, Louis handed me an envelope with ten thousand dollars in it, and he said, 'This is yours.' And I said, 'Why are you giving me this?' And he said, 'Because it's yours; it's your money. You brought people in. This is where you're at now. This is how much you should be making a week.' And I cried like a baby. Because I got ten thousand dollars for telling jokes, you know."

While it wasn't the first time the club had received mainstream notoriety, hearing it come from the mouth of someone who quite literally had the comedy world in the palm of his hand was a major seal of approval for Lee. And though the moment was fleeting, the history that led up to it went back more than fifteen years. "The first time Louis worked here was back in 1999," Lee recalls. "Mitch Hedberg brought in the whole 3 Arts crew when he did *Los Enchiladas!* It was Todd Barry, Louis, and a bunch of others. A lot of them did guest sets when they were here. Hedberg would tell me, 'Oh, you gotta see this guy and this guy.' I saw these guys do guest sets, and they were great."

C. K. became a regular addition to the Acme calendar, returning to town every year to perform. "Back in the early 2000s, shit was happening almost weekly with comics, waitstaff, the audience. And Louis would never stick around. He always kept his nose clean," Lee recalls. "One thing that kind of got me was that he didn't make a lot of money back then, but he'd pick a different hotel to stay at other than the normal one where most people would stay when they came. He was very private. Very nice, but when he's gone, he's gone."

After C. K.'s first major payday at Acme (at least major by his standards at that point in his career), Lee continued to support C. K. both in and out of the club, whether that meant vouching for him with other clubs and promoters, providing input about experiences with various agents and managers to help guide his career, or simply booking him during prime weeks out of the year. When C. K. first made the leap from performing in clubs to theaters locally, Acme would co-promote the shows, putting its full marketing and operations support behind the comic. By the time he sat down on the couch with Jimmy Fallon in 2015, C. K. was on top of the world, and hadn't forgotten those who helped him get there, as evidenced by his surprise show at Acme during the condo fight of 2016. But then, it all came undone.

In November 2017, the *New York Times* published allegations of sexual misconduct against C. K. by five different women, alleged to have taken place years earlier. C. K. released a response to the story, acknowledging his wrongdoing. He wrote, "These stories are true," before adding, "the power I had over these women is that they admired me. And I wielded that power irresponsibly." He concluded by stating, "I have spent my long and lucky career talking and saying anything I want. I will now step back and take a long time to listen."

The fallout to his admission was swift and severe. The release and distribution of his new movie was canceled. Both FX and Netflix cut ties with the comedian. And even his longtime manager Dave Becky and 3 Arts dropped C. K. as a client. "I saw how quickly everything got canceled," Lee says, reflecting on the free fall. "His movie was gone. His TV show was gone. Everyone around him got hurt."

In the aftermath, C. K. disappeared from the public eye. For a while, at least. In August the following year, C. K. made an unannounced appearance onstage at the Comedy Cellar in New York, performing for the first time publicly since his admission of guilt the previous year. The response from both fans and his fellow comics was mixed. While some, like comedy legends Dave Chappelle, Chris Rock, and Jerry Seinfeld, supported C. K.'s right to continue performing, others questioned whether his return was premature.

C. K. created even more controversy that December, when an audience member secretly recorded the comic as he worked out new material at a club show in Long Island. As was C. K.'s style, the material pushed boundaries and feigned anger for the sake of comedy. But jokes about school shootings threw gasoline on what was already a fiery debate about whether he should be allowed back onstage. "Testify in front of Congress, these kids, what the fuck? What are you doing?" C. K. asks the audience in the audio clip. "Because you went to a high school where kids got shot, why does that mean I have to listen to you? Why does that make you interesting? You didn't get shot. You pushed some fat kid in the way, and now I gotta listen to you talking?"

While some fans and comics took to social media to share their disgust over the material, which they felt mocked very real, very sensitive world issues like the Parkland school shooting that happened earlier the same year, Mike Earley, a local Twin Cities comic who had been working at Acme as an emcee since 2014, had a different perspective. "When the leaked set came out, it had been so long since I had actually heard comedy that I really looked up to, and I thought it was great," he explains. "I thought it was amazing. It was so fucking funny, and I forgot there was that level of quality out there."

Though the opinions about C. K., his comeback, and his material were being shared in every corner of the internet as well as in comedy clubs across America, C. K.'s in-person appearances had been confined to his home state of New York. But soon that would all change. Despite not having a close personal relationship, Lee and C. K. had maintained a level of professional respect dating back twenty years. So when C. K. started getting back onstage, Lee decided to relay a message of support back to his longtime colleague. "I had heard he was doing sets in New York," Lee recalls. "I had a comic friend who was tight with Louis, and I called him one day and asked how Louis was doing. He told me, 'He's trying to do stand-up.' I saw that, and I saw that he had lost everything, but that he also loves stand-up. So I told him, 'If you see Louis, tell him he can count on me.' That's when I got a call."

The call was from C. K.'s team, inquiring as to whether he could book some shows at Acme, the club that had changed his life just a few short years earlier. Without hesitation, Lee put him down for a week of shows. That May, Acme announced C. K.'s return to the club with eight performances, all of which would take place the following week. Immediately Acme and Lee became a lightning rod for media scrutiny, on both a local and a national level.

"Buy tickets to someone else," said Acme regular Emily Galati in a *Star Tribune* article just after the shows were announced. "There are plenty of comics who haven't sexually assaulted someone who you could support." Other national comics, including names like Nikki Glaser and Laurie Kilmartin, the latter of whom was a regular headliner at Acme, openly questioned why Lee would choose to bring C. K. to the club in light of his admission of misconduct and subsequent quick return to comedy.

Though many assumed Lee was blindly doing a favor for an old friend, he had taken the time to learn more about the issues and speak to others who had differing perspectives before making any decisions. "When he [C. K.] worked at Acme over the years, he worked with a lot of female comics locally, and I never had any issues," Lee recalls. "When everything came out, I dug deep into my contacts to where I was able to get the stories secondhand. I got close enough where I found people who had heard the stories directly from the women involved. After I heard everything, I took away three things: First, to me, he did an inappropriate thing. But so did 90 percent of comics back in those days. Second, if someone told him no, he would walk away. And third, I looked at the time frame. All of these incidents occurred in the late 1990s or early 2000s. Once he started to become more famous, when he would have had a lot more influence and power, none of that stuff came up."

While Lee was steadfast in his resolve to book C. K., the logic could be debated. Yes, C. K. had lost a great deal of professional opportunities and experienced financial repercussions. But for those who opposed the comic's return to Acme, the issue was less about whether he had been appropriately punished for his actions and more about the systemic issues in the comedy world—a world in which C. K. had formerly been at the top. Sure, the reported incidents had happened prior to his rise to fame, but many argued that the real issue wasn't the timeline of misdeeds, but rather the idea that Acme would be comfortable providing him a fresh opportunity, with no consideration for those who may have experienced similar situations at the club or other comedy rooms. In many ways, the conversation was less about C. K. being allowed to perform and more about the statement Acme was making as to whether comics who used poor judgment should be welcomed back home, especially given the number of comedians who were working to get the same opportunity and had not made similar flawed choices.

Despite the controversy, local fans of the comic were thrilled about his homecoming, buying up all 2,200 tickets across eight shows in just about six hours. The overwhelming response only intensified the local debate. Devohn Bland, a Twin Cities comedian who started his career in 2017 right before C. K. was canceled, recalls a mix of anger and uncertainty when it came to the feelings of those who opposed C. K. performing at Acme. "When I first saw the Louis C. K. [misconduct admission], my reaction was, *Aw shit, Louis?* He was fucking huge," Bland recalls. "I remember there was a big divide in the comedy community after that, and it was a conversation we had never really had before. Some people were like, 'Fuck him forever,' but others were out there saying, 'Yeah but he's inspired my comedy, so fuck him, but should he never get to do comedy again?' It was a very heated conversation that was boiling up, but when they announced he was coming to Acme it sort of brought it all to the surface. It was like, the monster is here. So what are we going to do about it?"

The debate about art, business, and sexual misconduct wasn't just happening among comics, comedy fans, and the media. It had consequences for service staff too. Hannah Rhodes was a server at Acme when the decision was made to bring in C. K. She says that soon after the announcement, the managers sat down with all the staff to check in and make any accommodations that felt necessary. "I remember the managers telling everyone on the staff, 'Louis C. K. is coming to perform here next week. If anyone doesn't feel comfortable working those shows, you don't have to. It's not a problem.' I appreciated how transparent they were with the staff, and every single person ended up working that week. But it was important to them that we were comfortable."

For the Acme shows, C. K. brought along his own opening acts—Joe List and Lynne Koplitz—both of whom were New York–based comics who had a strong working relationship with C. K. and who he knew would connect well with his audience. But C. K. decided he also wanted to utilize a local emcee for the week, and he reached out to Lee for his recommendation. "Originally it was going to be Slagle," Lee recalls, referring to his old friend and controversy magnet Tim Slagle. Lee's thought was that not only would Slagle mesh well with C. K. and his fan base but also he would be willing to tackle any media inquiries the club received leading up to the show. Unfortunately, Slagle accidentally double-booked himself the week of C. K.'s Acme shows, leaving Lee to look for a new opener. Enter Mike Earley.

Earley was a much younger comic in the scene, though he started performing comedy locally back in 2009. His sense of humor was dry and unassuming, but also delightfully dark, which made him a natural fit to take the opener slot for C. K. "I know Mike, and I know he won't care about anything people have to say to him," Lee says. "And he proved me right."

According to Earley, his invitation to open the shows stayed shrouded in secrecy prior to the announcement. Even to him. "I got a call from one of the Acme managers, asking if I was available to open for a comedian the following week,"

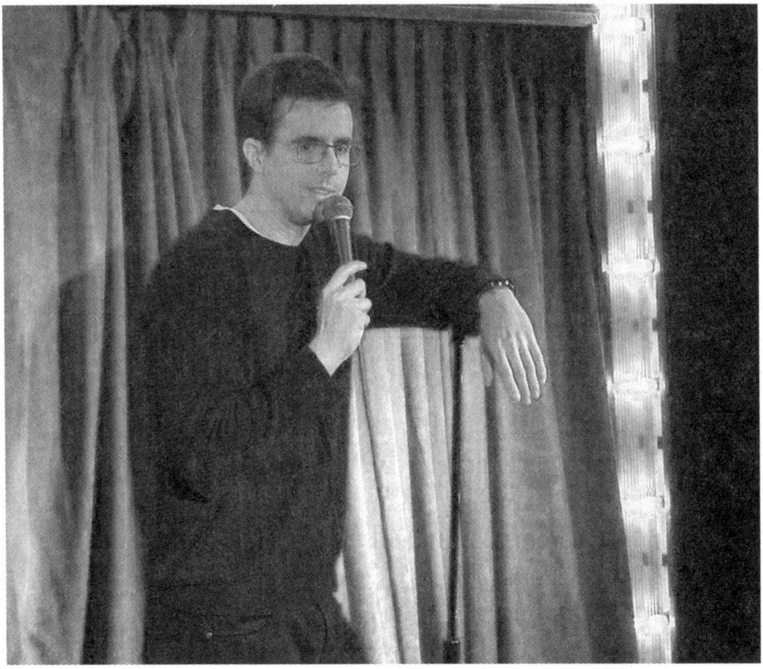

Comedian Mike Earley not only opened for Louis C. K. during his Acme shows but was later invited to go on tour with the comic. *Courtesy Acme Comedy Company*

Earley remembers. "It was like two shows Monday, two on Tuesday, two on Wednesday, and two on Thursday. It was all very kind of weird. I was like, 'Sure, I'll do it,' just trying to be cool or whatever. And then I'm wondering who it is. Because to be doing two shows a night on a Monday and Tuesday in Minnesota? There are only a few comics that could possibly do that." He believed there was a chance he would be opening for C. K., but he wasn't informed officially until just before the announcement went public and tickets went on sale. "This was a year after Louis was the biggest comedian in the world," Earley continues. "No one had really heard from him very much at that point, and he was larger than fucking life. So to be chosen to open for him was a very intense moment."

Earley was slightly disappointed, though, to learn he wasn't the club's first pick. "I felt like it was a big deal, but then I found out I was the second choice," he says. Even so, the opportunity was the biggest of Earley's career, and he knew it. While he and the people he was close with were ecstatic, some of the anger being directed toward C. K. came his way as well. "There was definitely this element of danger in the background," he recalls. "Everyone on Facebook, including people who weren't comics, were talking about how awful it was. So I put up a post and just said, 'I think he's the best comedian in the entire world, and I'm proud to be opening for him at Acme.' I felt pretty OK about that. It was interesting because a lot of people who seemed to be pretty publicly opposed to him coming to Acme were still pretty happy for me privately."

Not everyone was as understanding, however. In the days leading up to the shows, Earley endured numerous social media rants, insults, and lectures, chastising him for taking the gig. "I've gotten hate in the past for things I've performed, so I had already been through the wringer," he says. "When it came out that I was opening for Louis, it was just sort of like checking the weather. Like, *OK, today is the day that everyone hates me on the internet.*"

While Earley was used to being scrutinized by the public, the toughest criticisms were reserved for Lee. He made a rare TV appearance, in an interview with local NBC affiliate KARE 11, where he was questioned about his motives as well as his own moral code. "It was bad," Lee recalls about the media scrutiny. "Everyone wanted to try and decide what kind of punishment he deserves. They want to play God. I'm not God, so I'm not doing that. I told Jana [Shortal, the journalist who interviewed Lee] that he had lost his other creative outlets, and she admitted that she didn't know that. I give her credit because she kept that part in."

During the interview, Lee said he had spoken to local comedians, primarily women, and was able to get their opinion on C. K. returning to the club, admitting that they were upset with him over the decision. "Before I even got the call about bringing him to the club, I had dinner with a comic who I like a lot," Lee recalls. "We started talking about Louis, and I said, 'If I get a call, I'll say yes.' And she said, 'Why?' And I told her all about how I looked into it, and then I asked her, 'Is that [the] sickest thing you've ever heard about a comic?' She agreed with that, but she told me the only way she could ever be OK with him performing is if he apologizes onstage for what he did. I told her that he did apologize privately, but there's no way he's going to do it onstage. I asked her, 'If someone told you what to say when you got onstage, as a comic, would you do it?' And she said, 'No, I'd probably do the opposite.' She came around a little and said she would be curious to see how he would approach it onstage. And I told her that we'll never know if someone doesn't give him the chance to do a full set."

Other comics were not convinced. As time ticked by and C. K.'s arrival at the club drew closer, some decided they weren't going to stand idly by without making their voices heard. And not just online. Madeleine Farley was early in her stand-up comedy career when she heard the news of C. K.'s return to Acme. She had been familiar with the murmurings surrounding the comic for years prior to the publication of the allegations. "I had heard about the danger that Louis C. K. posed to women as far back as when I was a teenager reading feminist blogs and news sites," she recalls. "His 'open secret' is something that made me uninterested in watching and performing comedy for a long time."

When the rumors were publicly confirmed by C. K., Farley says she was relieved and hoped he would be punished. "When his actions became more widely recognized and the allegations accepted as true—he had spent years violently refuting them and inciting his fans to do likewise—it did feel like some small justice had been done. But I knew he would always have fans, always have money, and always have power. My reaction was mostly just, *Fucking finally*. It also felt like maybe in the future people would be afraid to do what he did if he ever saw consequences for it."

So when she heard that C. K. would be performing eight sold-out shows at Acme, right in her own backyard, Farley was, to put it lightly, pissed off. "I was furious. Like, raging," she says. "I was so pissed because it felt like it would be the easiest thing in the world to not hire him. One of the most cut-and-dry examples of violence that was proven in the mostly unfulfilled Me Too movement, and still he's playing sold-out shows. I was blistering with anger. Not just because one of the only 'real' comedy clubs in the area was hosting him, but that I had to have what felt like conversation after conversation with my fellow comedians as to why this was unacceptable and should be heavily critiqued by us as the local community. People I thought were cool seemed to give both Acme and Louis C. K. the benefit of the doubt. Ultimately it was very disgusting to see people defend Louis C. K. and Acme for booking him."

At that point, Farley decided she needed to act. She organized protests to take place outside the club, and invited her fellow comedians, artists, social activists, and concerned citizens to join in the demonstrations to be held the week C. K. was at the club. It was new, uncharted territory for Acme, which until that point had been mostly applauded for its commitment to supporting controversial comics.

People began to speculate as to just *why* Lee would allow C. K. to return to the club. Was it strictly a financial decision? Was it loyalty to an old friend? Even during his interview with KARE 11, Lee was asked, "Did you agree to host Louis C. K. this week because he did so many things that were kind to Acme? Or because you believe he deserves a second chance as a comic?" To which he simply answered, "Both." But anyone who may have thought his motivations were skewed by friendship, he says, would be mistaken. "Louis isn't a guy who I would go out to dinner and have drinks with when he came to town," explains Lee. "All along, I respected him, and he knew that. He appreciates how this room works. While he was on top, he wrote some things on his website and said after he'd work here, he'd feel energized. He always had really nice things to say about Acme." Lee continues, "I stood up for him, even though we aren't close, and he knew I'd stand up for him and all the comics. I look at him as a person who, as an artist, is doing what I want to see. It's purely professional. He, to me, already got enough punishment. At that time, people just wanted to finish him off. That's why there was so much hatred toward me and the club. And I didn't care."

After weeks of discussion, the shows finally arrived. Farley, true to her word, led a small but passionate group of protestors outside the club, engaging in conversations with audience members who were flocking to get a glimpse of a superstar as he began his reascension. Unsurprisingly, the reactions to the protestors were mixed. "There weren't a ton of people that showed up. Probably less than ten each day," recalls Bland. "Going to the protest taught me a lot about the audience he brings in. Some people were just diehard Louis C. K. fans. We talked to them, and they were like, 'Hey, we're glad you're protesting. I just want to see what he says.' With other people it was like talking to an R. Kelly fan or a Michael Jackson fan. They're like, 'Yeah, he's gross, but I love his stuff so much and I grew up with it. I can't help it.' But then there was a level of, like, alt-right people who showed up. Just a bunch of Karens who were very aggressive to the protestors. We had trans people protesting and people were saying transphobic stuff to them. We had more women than men at the protest, and there were some very misogynist things said. And these things are being said to us by people who paid money to see Louis C. K. perform. After a while, it was like we're protesting Louis C. K., but it became a bigger thing. Like you had one group of people pretending nothing happened, and another group that knew what happened and were mad at us for giving a shit. They'd say stuff like, 'Boo hoo some people got touched or jerked off at or whatever. So what? He's still funny as hell.' "

While representatives from the club, including Lee, didn't engage with the protest, they had no issue with the protestors' presence. Earley even went outside and talked with the group for a few minutes before the first show of the week kicked off, in order to better understand their purpose. "I was confused," Earley recalls of his interaction with the protestors. "[The protest] was comedians I had seen at open mics and stuff like that, and people acted like there was this big schism in the local scene over these shows, but then it was only like six people. The whole thing just seemed kind of silly to me."

While his interaction outside was tense, inside the club Earley was eager to meet the man of the hour. "It's kind of surreal because you've seen him on TV forever, and now he's standing in front of you," he remembers of his first interaction with C. K. "I just shook his hand and told him I was honored to meet him, and then I did my job and hung out."

When Earley first took the stage, he quickly addressed the elephant in the room. "Thank you all for coming in tonight," he said as he opened his set. "Who knew that coming to a comedy show on a Monday would feel like walking into an abortion clinic in Iowa?" The audience was overwhelmingly receptive and ready to support C. K., and the shows went off without a hitch. That said, Earley himself admits that the crowd was a little different than the usual Acme clientele.

"It was a Monday night of drinking in Minnesota," Earley laughs. "There was definitely an element of sloppiness. It was kind of rowdy. I think in general Minnesotans don't know how to be out on a weekday. It was like that for the late shows too. I think people treated it like they could bilk out another day of the weekend. I mean, the shows were great. They were a little drunker, maybe a little sloppier than a weekend show. With big acts like that, it can be harder to win the crowd over initially because there's this element of, like, *Alright, we came here to see him. When is he coming out?* But overall, I'd say it was just a lot of excitement and intoxication."

Despite having a harder time winning over the crowd in front of the curtain during the week, Earley was unknowingly gaining a few new fans behind it. "Apparently one of the first nights when I was onstage, Louis was the first one to tune in," Earley recalls. "He asked Joe and Lyn, 'Have you heard this guy?' and then I guess they were all behind the curtain listening to me. It was super flattering when I found out. It was just pretty fucking great that Louis was listening to me before anyone else."

Still, Earley says he did his best to maintain boundaries throughout the week. "I didn't try to interject with my funny quips or anything like that," he laughs. "I didn't try to nut ride or be a part of the gang. My job was just to be the best emcee I could be while still thinking, like, *This is fucking amazing*." Before the second-to-last show, however, Earley was invited into the circle. "I was treating the whole experience like, if it happens one time, it's amazing," he says. "Then on that second-to-last day, Louis started talking to me and asking how long I'd been doing comedy. Then everyone was talking about people getting upset about pet jokes, and I told them my joke about how my friend got a rescue dog and I saw it for the first time and was like, 'Hey, that's my old dog.' And everyone laughed, and I was just like, *Hell yeah*."

What Earley didn't know was that C. K. had been discussing with List and Koplitz whether he should invite Earley to come out on the road as one of his opening acts. The comics agreed that Earley had the chops to join the group, and that's when C. K. extended a career-changing invite. "He said, 'Hey, are you free for the next couple of weeks? Can you come to Nashville next week?' I mean, I had to tell my framing construction job that I needed time off, but they understood the deal."

While the invitation may have shocked Earley, Lee says his history with C. K. left him unsurprised at the comic's act of support. "Louis doesn't have to care about who emceed that show," Lee explains. "He brought his own people. But he cared enough about comedy that he watched Mike and decided to bring him along on the road."

The shows were a success for the club, which brought C. K. back again in 2021, and for Earley, who spent the next several months traveling the country as one of C. K.'s opening acts. But the event left others in the local comedy scene dejected and upset, creating wounds that still exist today. "I saw a lot of people in the comedy scene lose hope," recalls Bland. "There were people who worked at Acme who kind of had to defend the decision of the club, and I felt sad that they did that. In the moment, I was filled with a feeling of defeat. We protested, but he had eight sold-out shows. I don't think we 'won' in terms of trying to get audience members not to support him, but I do think we succeeded by having an important conversation in the comedy scene about this space we perform in and what we expect from them and what we won't tolerate. We didn't have a lot of people protesting, but it needed to be known that *some* comics protested. Acme is an important club. I've performed with people who have traveled the country, and they talk about wanting to do Acme. They have an important responsibility to the scene, and they have a huge responsibility to do the right thing. In my personal opinion they didn't do the right thing in that particular instance."

Lee came away with the satisfaction of believing that the results had once again vindicated his gut instincts when others thought he was making the wrong choice. "For someone who was going through all of this stuff and still trying to come back, he proved to me that he loved comedy as much as anyone, and I respect that," Lee says. "When that week was over and I could honestly look at him and see how much he cares about comedy, I knew I made a good call. All that shit I ate, I took it, and it was worth it."

Regardless of anyone's feelings about the decision to bring C. K. back to the club, the event showed Lee to be someone who values loyalty. His argument was based on a principle. He supported those who had supported him. But many others, be they comedians, comedy fans, or victims of abuse, argued that loyalty shouldn't be an excuse to gloss over poor behavior. The situation also forced both Lee and those who looked at Acme as a home to accept that the club was still a business, and that being a business owner means balancing—or sometimes choosing between—personal and professional beliefs. Was Lee right to allow C. K. back? Should he have banished the comic forever? To this day, the debate has never been resolved. What cannot be questioned is that Lee made a decision and stuck with it in the face of controversy.

· CHAPTER 14 ·

BETS, FIGHTS, AND NATURAL DISASTERS

While there have been a number of defining moments in the life of Acme Comedy Company, from Robin Williams personally requesting to perform at the club in 2008 as he prepared for his comeback stand-up comedy special to Tim Slagle reuniting with his biological mother for the very first time inside the club, a litany of insane, hilarious, shocking, and bizarre moments have played just as big a role in shaping Acme's history. Here are a few of those moments, told by the people who lived them.

Sarah Drew: Comedy doesn't take a snow day

Part of the reason comedy thrives in Minnesota is because it gives people something to laugh about during the brutally cold half of the year. Back in 2010, however, the conditions nearly became too intense for Acme to handle. "We had Tom Segura headlining back during the blizzard of 2010," Drew recalls. "We got something like twenty inches of snow, and I remember getting stuck three times on my drive into work. That night, there were literally six of us, three of which were the comedians. All of a sudden, fifty people showed up, all with southern accents. They were just like, 'This is what the weather is like in Minnesota, right?' "

While some would have panicked, Drew and company dug deep, juggling multiple jobs and making the show just as good for those fifty people on that night as it would have been in the dead of summer with three hundred people and a full staff. "Tom killed," she says. "He said it was one of the best sets of his life. I remember he got to like the fifty-minutes mark and yelled to me from the stage, 'Hey Sarah, should I keep going or should I fuck off?' And I was like, 'Fuck off, Tom. We're going to be sleeping here if you don't get off the stage soon.' But it felt really good to see how we all came together to make that night a success."

Rich Miller: Talk softly and carry a big knife

Even after Rich Miller was no longer living in Minnesota, he and Louis Lee had developed a close enough relationship that Miller would pitch in at the club from time to time. Usually that meant keeping the show moving, helping out the bartenders, or managing the occasional unruly audience member. One night, however, Miller got more than he bargained for. "I remember Louis lost one of his managers right before his big banquet season, which is like the end of November through January," Miller recalls. "He called me and asked if I'd give him a hand, so I said sure. I really didn't want to be out on the floor, but he's a friend, so I figured what the hell."

There must have been something in the air that holiday season, because according to Miller he had an unusually large number of people who needed to be shown the door. "I threw out so many drunks that year," he laughs. "They flocked to me. One night I threw out a group of forty guys. It was a big bachelor party. They came in on a bus, and they were already drunk. They were giving one of the waitresses a lot of shit, so I actually stopped the whole show and told them, 'All of you guys are out of here.' "

While tossing a group of drunks would be nerve-racking for anyone, Miller says there was one particular patron who really struck some fear into his heart. "One night, I threw out a biker and his girlfriend," he recalls. "And they went nuts. He's threatening me, she's screaming at the staff, and we're just trying to push them out the door. In the middle of all of this, I look up and I see Louis in the doorway by the kitchen, and he's staring at us and sharpening the biggest butcher's knife I've ever seen. I had to stop and catch myself. I'm thinking I have to try to throw this guy out, and I'm most worried I'm going to start laughing. Like, *Louis, what are you going to do with that?*"

On that night, Lee didn't actually get involved in the confrontation physically. But on some nights he found himself in the thick of all the chaos.

John DeBoer: "Please stop elbowing me"

John DeBoer couldn't catch a break at Acme during the pandemic. His shows were canceled twice due to the mandatory curfew that was implemented in the wake of protests following the murder of George Floyd, as well as by a second wave of COVID cases that forced shutdowns around the holidays.

Finally, he was able to have a show at his home club. But even that one almost didn't happen. "My aunt and my mom came to the show that night, and when they first got there they overheard a very large man in a hoodie outside talking to his friends about how he was going to fuck with the comics," DeBoer recalls. "So they told me, and I told one of the employees to watch out for them. Sure enough, not five minutes into the feature act and these guys are all throwing popcorn at each other."

Already on high alert, the staff member told the gentleman that he needed to leave. That's when all hell broke loose.

"Hannah [Rhodes, one of the Acme managers] told me that someone was throwing popcorn, and I was like, 'We don't even serve popcorn!'" remembers Brandon Simon, one of the *several* managers and employees who got involved in the ruckus. "So I go running towards the door, and I see Joe [Feely, a third Acme manager] and another one of the employees trying to drag this guy out. And he punches Joe right in the face."

Always quick to protect their own, the bartenders and other managers came rushing to aid in the situation. "I see the bartenders running over, and I figure it must be going down," laughs DeBoer. "And they start dogpiling on this guy. Every manager is in on it, Hannah is smacking him, and then all of a sudden Louis jumps on top." Simon adds, "He did this move where he double-tapped his elbow and then started elbow smashing the guy in the back. Finally the guy stops fighting and just calmly says, 'Whoever is elbowing me in the back, can you please stop?'"

The situation resolved itself quickly after that, but the legend of Lee and his deadly elbows began to grow. "That next week, Cy Amundson [a longtime Acme comic] called me up. He didn't even say hello when I answered the phone. He just goes, 'He double-tapped his elbow? How did I miss this?'"

Nick Swardson: How many shots is too many?

Despite leaving for New York and becoming a major star in both stand-up as well as movies and television, Nick Swardson always made a point to return to Acme as much as possible. And whenever he did, he was welcomed back with open arms. Usually. "Pretty early on in my career I came back to town to do shows on my birthday weekend one year," recalls Swardson. "I had Zach Galifianakis with me as my opener, and I was just in a really good mood."

Not one to turn down an excuse to party, Swardson decided to start celebrating that night from the stage. "I'm in my mid-twenties and being dumb, so I grab a waitress while I'm onstage and I say, 'Can I get seven shots of tequila?' And they were all for me. Then I look out into the crowd, and they're all kind of giving me this look like, *Whoa*. I realized that was sort of a loose cannon move, so I tried to cover real quick and said, 'Does anybody want to do a shot with me onstage?' And it became chaos."

Suddenly, the typically well-behaved Acme crowd went riotous, hopping onstage with drinks and shots, toasting their hometown hero and throwing the show into complete disarray. "It was the most stupid thing I could possibly do," Swardson laughs. "It was like such an Iggy Pop thing. I remember I saw Iggy Pop one time and he invited people up onstage and it just became a complete disaster. That's pretty much what happened that night at Acme. Honestly, I think it was one of my favorite moments ever."

Even the managers, who had grown accustomed to all sorts of insanity happening around the club, were none too impressed. "They gave me this look from the back of the room like, *Nick? No. Come on, man*. But I didn't feel bad. There's no rules in comedy."

Louis Lee: The most cutthroat gambler in all of comedy

If you step into the back office at Acme, you'll notice some unusual decorations covering the walls. Framed photos of various comedians with handwritten messages calling out their own stupidity, snapshots of grown men dressed in wildly embarrassing outfits, and a handful of dollar bills all serve as trophies of bets between Louis and various comedians throughout the years.

While plenty of comedians have challenged Lee, there is one who just couldn't take enough of a beating from the Acme owner: Cy Amundson. Amundson, a diehard Minnesota Vikings fan, pledged his undying allegiance to the purple his entire life. While some would look at this dedication as endearing, Lee saw it as an opportunity for humiliation. "The first year that [Brett] Favre played for the Vikings, we placed a bet that they would win a championship," Lee recalls. "Then when they lost, Cy had to write a letter explaining how I was right about everything, and that he was wrong."

While that outcome was fairly innocuous, Amundson and Lee decided to up the ante the following year. "The next season, he bet me that the Vikings would go 12–4. When they didn't, he had to wear an Aaron Rodgers jersey onstage and fellate bananas," Lee laughs. Allegedly there is video evidence of this bet locked away in the Acme safe, a fact Amundson is likely all too aware of.

While most people would have walked away after two consecutive years of abuse, Amundson was a glutton for punishment and made yet another bet with Lee the following season. "He bet me that the Vikings were going to go to the Super Bowl, and they lost again," Lee laughs maniacally. "This time, the deal was that he had to get up on a Monday night at the open mic and let the other comics roast him. Instead, they held an intervention onstage for his gambling problem."

While Amundson was a favorite target, Lee has won bets with comics, bartenders, and Acme managers, and he always comes to collect his winnings. One year he made a bet with comedian Tommy Ryman, with Ryman placing his faith in the Minnesota Vikings to win the Super Bowl. Had Ryman won, Lee would have been forced to pay him a thousand dollars. But he didn't win. And the price was steep.

On January 31, 2023, Ryman was scheduled to be the closing act for Acme's open mic night. But he wouldn't be performing his own jokes. Instead, he would be performing a very special comedy set written by his fellow comics at Lee's behest. "Tonight we have a special set," said comedian Mike Lester from the stage. "The bet was that the Minnesota Vikings would win the Super Bowl. Which is a shitty bet. But before we bring up

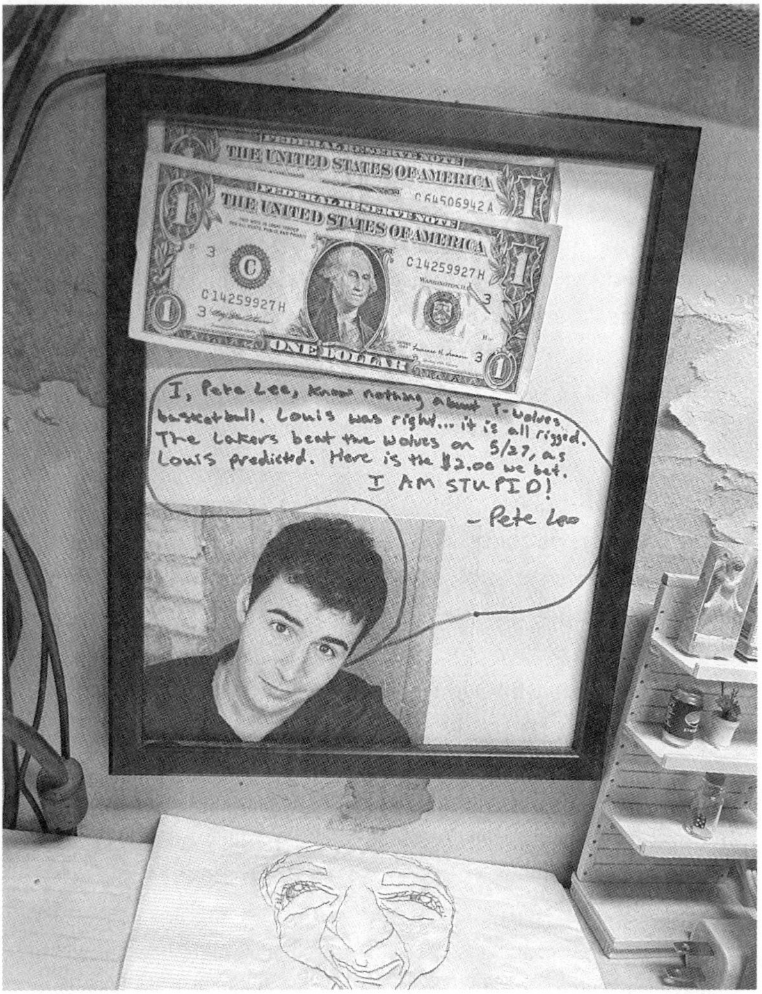

Pete Lee is just one of many comics who have mistakenly placed bets with Louis Lee. *Courtesy Patrick Strait*

Tommy to pay his debt, we have a few special videos." Past bet losers Amundson and Pete Lee appeared on screen chastising Ryman for his poor decision-making. "What are you doing?" said Lee. "You don't bet with Louis. He will dominate you. Welcome to the Don't Bet Against Louis Club."

"I know exactly what you're going through, and exactly what you're feeling," Amundson added in his video. "If you're going to continue to bet with the Dragon, I think I can give some advice. He doesn't care about money. This is a man who deals in power."

Finally, Ryman took the stage to perform a set written by Bryan Miller and Nate Abshire. Immediately, Ryman had to pop off his shirt onstage, revealing a collection of gold chains draped across his body and abs drawn on with a marker. And that was just the start. Over the next several minutes, Ryman, who has carved out a niche as a clean comic and has racked up hundreds of thousands of views on his YouTube specials, had to rattle off hacky jokes about women, Irish people, and COVID vaccines, before finishing it off by humping a stool onstage.

"In conclusion, I was wrong and Louis Lee was right," Ryman said at the end of the set. "Looking back, I haven't been this wrong since I fed my dog a chocolate bar to cheer him up."

• CHAPTER 15 •

NOT DEAD YET

As 2020 rolled around, Acme looked to be in a position to continue its success as the premier destination for stand-up comedy in Minnesota—and had also started making big plans to help take things to another level. In December 2019, Lee decided to invest a significant amount of money in having high-definition recording equipment installed inside the club. The intent, he says, was so that comedians could film clips, or even full specials, with the same three-camera setup as a major production company. "I wanted to give the locals the ability to film themselves and send those clips out to get jobs," Lee explains.

While he didn't have any firm plans in place for what to do with his new investment, Lee had inadvertently made a move that would save his club, and potentially comedy in Minnesota along with it. New technology notwithstanding, Acme continued to do what it did best: bring in the best comedians in the country, develop new talent, and nurture its audience to maintain its well-earned reputation as a must-see comedy destination.

A-list comics like Jon Dore and Laurie Kilmartin sold out the club during the first couple of months of the year. Hometown hero Chad Daniels sold out a full week of shows, signaling that he was ready to make the leap from club shows to theaters in Minnesota. Up-and-comers like Mike Earley ascended to headliner status for the first time. And legends like Bobcat Goldthwait booked returns to the club for the first time in many, many years. All systems were go for Acme to have one of its best years ever. And then, everything stopped.

When the term *coronavirus* started gaining traction in early 2020, no one could have predicted what it would do to the world as a whole, let alone the live entertainment industry. So when word began to circulate in mid-March that the virus had made its way to the United States, and events like NBA basketball games and concerts started getting canceled, the management at Acme knew they were on borrowed time. "We would all just be standing around in the bar watching TV, wondering when they were going to tell us we had to close," says Hannah Rhodes, one of Acme's three managers at the time.

One of the other managers, Brandon Simon, had been a part of Acme for five years at that point, and believed he had seen just about everything when it came to live comedy. But the week before things shut down, Simon admits he had no clue how to handle the uncertainty. "We had Jake Johannsen at the club the week stuff started shutting down," he says. "And I remember Thursday morning I was driving him to a radio interview at KQRS. I think it was the morning after the NBA had stopped mid-game and postponed the season, and Jake looked at me and goes, 'Are we stupid for doing this?' And I just had to be like, 'I have no idea.' No one knew."

When Johannsen completed his weekend of shows at Acme that Saturday night, it would be the last time the club had a full audience for over a year. "That Monday we were watching TV in the bar during the open mic, and they announced we were shutting down the next day," says Joe Feely, the third Acme manager at the time. "I really felt like, *Is this it? Are we ever going to open back up again? Or is this going to be like a past form of entertainment that isn't going to exist anymore?*"

For the next week or so, Lee, the managers, and the staff

sat in limbo, waiting to see what would happen next, and hoping they would get word that they could go back to work. For the comics, who had spent years grinding away onstage and on the road, making their living from their creativity and ability to connect with audiences, the shutdown left their entire lives in a state of uncertainty.

"When that first initial wave of shutdowns happened, I personally felt the blow," says Greg Coleman, who had been an integral part of Acme and the Minnesota comedy scene since 2012. "That week before, I was out in New York having meetings. I had a general meeting with a streaming service, met with potential representation, a talent agency. It just felt like a lot of the things I had been working towards were finally starting to come to fruition. Before I came back home, I had people being like, 'Let's see about getting you on *Conan*!' And then everything just stopped."

While Coleman felt opportunity slipping through his fingers, other comics like Bryan Miller chose to approach the situation with a more optimistic outlook. "I mean, my first reaction was that I didn't want to die. I didn't want my family to die. But honestly I was a little Polyannaish about the whole thing," Miller admits. "I was doing shows right up until the lockdown happened. I remember I was in Chicago doing shows that weekend, and everything still felt pretty normal. Then that Saturday afternoon the police came through and shut down the whole Loop. That's when it really started to set in."

Despite assurances that people would have to stay inside for just two short weeks, comics quickly began to surmise that this period of lockdown might last longer than advertised. And some began to take action. "I started doing shows on Zoom three days after the lockdown started," says Jackie Kashian. The longtime Acme favorite was living in California by then and recalls the first time she realized COVID wouldn't be a short-term issue.

"I remember when we heard the news [about the shutdown]

and no one knew what it was going to be like," she continues. "We thought maybe it would last like two weeks, or maybe even two months. But the vibe I got when I was flying back from Indiana on March 15, when there was almost no one in the airports, and the people who were there were completely freaked out, was you're out of your mind if you think this is going to be over in two months. So at that point, I just knew I had to find a way to do comedy."

Kashian was one of the early adopters of Zoom comedy, broadcasting live from her office daily for any audience she could muster up. One day it was a private show for a fan she had connected with four years earlier through Snapchat. The next, a birthday set for an eighty-five-year-old woman. "I am not a scientist, I am not a health professional. I am a clown," she said in an interview with the *Star Tribune*. "I can do my job, which is hopefully to keep people up, to cheer people up a little bit."

Meanwhile at Acme, Lee had an idea on how to put his new cameras to work, while helping the comics who desperately needed it. "I decided we would do a Zoom show of our own to raise money for the comics," Lee explains. "I opened it up to any Acme headliner or feature. I think some of the emcees too. Anyone who wanted to participate was invited, but if anyone felt uncomfortable that was OK." On March 26, Acme presented its first-ever live stream show, taking place inside the club, for an audience you could count on two hands. Fortunately, Lee's broadcast equipment investment of just a few months earlier helped give the appearance that they had been pumping out comedy over the internet for years.

"We recorded from the completely empty club," recalls Miller, who performed the show alongside Coleman, plus fellow comics John DeBoer, Corey Adam, Robert Baril, Ahmed Khalaf, Mike Earley, and James Moore. "I think he charged like fifteen dollars for it, and whatever profits he got he split that evenly amongst the comics."

Greg Coleman was one of the Acme regulars who recorded a Zoom show in front of a (mostly) empty showroom at the start of the pandemic.
Courtesy Brandon Simon

The show itself was a welcome distraction from the uncertainty in the world, though the changes were notable. Rhodes served as the cleaner, wiping down mic stands between each set, while some comics chose to wear latex gloves, as the information about how the virus was passed was not yet known. Still, the spirit of the club and comics who brought it to life was as strong as ever.

"Louis finally solved the parking problem!" DeBoer laughed as he opened his set. Approximately five hundred people purchased the special, and Lee cut checks to all the comics who participated, not keeping a single dime for himself. "It was several hundred dollars," recalls Miller. "Louis has done so many amazing things for comics over the years, to the point you almost get used to it. But for Louis to do that in a time when zero money was coming in was so helpful. And for me, I just remember that getting to do kind of a regular show on the stage at Acme was so nice."

The show was the last performance of any kind in the club for the next several months. "We were all in such good spirits, just getting to do any sort of a show," recalls Rhodes. Adds Feely, "It was fun, but it felt sort of like a send-off. Like when we were stacking up chairs at the end, it sort of felt like that might be the last time." Despite the sense of uncertainty, Feely says, the show also served as a reminder of the closeness of the Acme employees, both past and present. "There was a live chat during the show," he says. "That part was really reassuring. There were comics and even a bunch of the old ushers and servers who were joining in. It was super bittersweet."

Businesses of all sizes began laying off employees, or in some cases shutting their doors for good, but Lee worked to find ways to keep his staff afloat. "We would have meetings in the empty club every afternoon," recalls Simon. "It would be the four of us, sitting in a circle, with like ten feet in between us." Despite the fact that there was no indication as to when customers might be able to return to the club, Lee continued to pay his staff in order to help maintain their livelihoods. "Louis was very generous," recalls Simon. "He kept us on the payroll, plus he would pay the kitchen staff to come in and clean. Really, just anything he could think of to give them hours. From the beginning, he was very giving and transparent."

"He actually started to get really vulnerable with us," Feely recalls, as the group collectively chokes up at the memory. "He was worried about how the pandemic was impacting us mentally, and wanted to do whatever he could to make sure we were taking care of ourselves. It was a really close moment for all of us and showed us the character of the person we were working for."

Weekly Zoom meetings were held with Lee and all the staff, in order to continue boosting morale and to maintain a level of normalcy in an extremely abnormal time. All the while, Lee continued to reassure the staff that Acme wasn't going anywhere. "We never got the vibe from him that he was going to pull the plug," says Feely. "It was more like, how long is this going to last?" Adds Rhodes, "He would tell the staff that he wanted us to stick with him and with Acme through COVID and be here when we reopened."

While the business side of Acme was put on pause, the creative side couldn't be contained. Local comics had begun hosting Zoom comedy shows, and Kashian herself was beginning to draw a decent crowd for her weekly (or sometimes nightly) performances. With no signs of a vaccine or a reopening on the horizon, comedy clubs soon started reaching out to Kashian to discuss hosting Zoom shows of their own. But there was only one club she was interested in working with. "I called Louis and said, 'If you want to do this, I will host it,'" she recalls. "I know you have the equipment, and I know the four of you are just spookily walking around that empty building." Always willing to try new things, Lee jumped on the opportunity and scheduled the first Acme Comedy Company Zoom Showcase for Saturday, April 25, with Kashian, along with Acme mainstays Tommy Ryman and Andy Erikson.

The demand was overwhelming, and much like a prepandemic Saturday night, the first show sold out quickly, and a second Zoom show was added. The format was different, but for the comics, the ability to perform with Acme was a welcome reprieve. "I've done so many weird shows in my career that honestly, the Zoom shows just felt like another weird show," laughs Kashian. "I've done shows in a hat store, a cornfield; I've done a show next to a whorehouse in Australia. Zoom shows were just another weird show. But being able to see the Acme regulars was so soothing. Being a part of that and seeing some of the staff and the comics, I was like, *Home club! That's my home club!* and it just felt reassuring. The other great thing about those shows was that whoever was performing, I knew they weren't sick."

Acme's Zoom shows became a way to connect with audiences during the pandemic, with comics like Jackie Kashian, Erica Rhodes, and John DeBoer performing from home. *Courtesy Brandon Simon*

In the coming weeks, nearly every Acme alum logged on to take part in the Zoom shows. Pete Lee, Tim Harmston, Mary Mack, and more logged on for an audience of roughly three hundred people per show—the same as a sold-out night inside of Acme—and performed for a small but mighty smattering of laughs through their computer speakers.

Greg Coleman participated in one of these shows as well, though he admits it wasn't the beacon of hope for him that it was for other comics. "Those first Zoom shows were tough because no one really knew how to do it," he remembers. "But eventually we got it figured out and it was like, at least we have an audience. At least people will pay five or ten dollars or whatever it was for a Zoom link. But to me, it was bleak. It felt bleak as someone who loves being in the room."

As with the show recorded at the club at the start of the pandemic, Lee once again made sure all the profits went to the comics. "Louis wanted to do those Zoom shows for the same reason he ridiculously opened a comedy club," laughs Kashian. "Because he loves comedy. One of the greatest things about Louis is that he loves a new idea. I knew it was driving him nuts not having live comedy, so when the idea came along he was like, *I'll try that*. And when he gets excited about a new idea, he's going to throw a little bit of money or a medium amount of money or a whole lot of money at it. It wasn't about the money for him. So no, he wasn't going to take a few hundred bucks away from the performers. He wanted to spread it around as much as he could."

The Zoom shows were unique for obvious reasons, but something else happened during the second week of shows that no one could have anticipated: Louis Lee got onstage. Well, the virtual stage, at least. "Louis tells us near the end of the show that he was going to make an announcement," recalls Simon. "So like right at the end of the show, there were maybe like fifty or sixty people left, and Louis pops up and says something like, 'We're going to reopen as soon as possible.' It was really surprising. That's how I could tell he really cared."

After a few weeks of Kashian hosting Zoom shows, Acme decided it was time to kick things up a notch, and planned to start broadcasting live shows from inside the club. The "live" audience would only consist of the management and fellow comics, but the idea of getting comics back onstage with a real microphone in hand signaled another step in the right direction. An article in the *Star Tribune* on May 29, 2020, trumpeted the return of a slightly more live comedy experience, with John DeBoer scheduled to be the first to test the new system that weekend. Unfortunately, he never got the chance.

When George Floyd was murdered by police in Minneapolis on May 25, it set off protests, riots, and an uprising that engulfed the city for the next several days. As a result, the city announced a mandatory curfew for that weekend, in an effort to curb the destruction and potentially prevent more violence. While the comics, staff, and audiences were disappointed, the curfew and forced closure of the club pushed Lee to the brink. "I was just so angry with everything," Lee recalls. "The whole city was burning, the pandemic was still going, and I just felt like all of this was never going to end. It wasn't the money, either. For me it was that I had no control over my own business. I worked hard to build this, and now I felt like it was being taken from me. That's when I said I'm done."

While he never broadcast the fact that he intended to close the club, in his mind the decision was final. Acme had hosted its final show, and the comedy institution that had defined Minnesota for nearly three decades had reached its end. The only thing left to do was tell his family. "I sat my daughter down and said, 'I'm done and I'm out.' And she asked me why. I told her that I'd had enough of the BS. She thought about it for a minute and asked, 'Are we going to lose our house?' And I said, 'No.' Then she asked me, 'Are we going to be OK?' And I told her, 'Probably. We aren't going to starve.' Then she asked me a few other questions, and then she said something like, 'So you're just not going to fight anymore?' I don't think it was quite that direct, but I took it that way. That got through to me. I had to take a second when she said that. That's when I looked at her and was like, 'You know what? I'll think about it.' I don't know that this was how she meant it, but her question leads me to believe that she's saying, 'So you're going to let these people tell you what to do with your business?' And I say to myself, *No. Fuck it. I'm going to do it.*"

Through a stroke of serendipity, in the days that followed Lee's decision to keep going, the announcement was made that businesses would be allowed to reopen, albeit with extremely limited capacities and a litany of strict regulations. "I think we were given like one week's notice," Simon recalls. "Businesses could reopen starting on a Wednesday, and we did our first shows that next week."

Preparing the club to reopen was no small feat. The managers and staff sprang into action, following the state-mandated safety protocol checklist to a T—even when the changes didn't always make sense. "We put up plexiglass in front of the box office," recalls Rhodes. "And then we had plexiglass dividers that we built that we put on each side of the tables." The club laid down floor markers to ensure patrons remained six feet apart, servers were instructed to wear gloves, place food on trays, and walk six feet away while serving customers in the restaurant. The managers began an exhaustive hunt to find as much hand sanitizer as possible. "We finally got some from a distillery in town," Rhodes recalls. "It was just hilarious how hard it was to find. When we did find it, it smelled like stale tequila."

The most noticeable change, however, was the limited seating capacity. According to state regulations, businesses could operate at 25 percent capacity. In the case of Acme, this rule meant the usually packed three-hundred-person showroom was limited to just seventy-five seats. But for Lee and the Acme managers and staff who hadn't had a single person walk through their doors in three months, seventy-five people might as well have been a stadium of fans. But the truly encouraging part of the reopening for the comics was seeing that Lee wasn't going down without a fight. "I remember ten or twelve years ago, Louis was thinking of opening a second club," recalls Kashian. "And when he decided not to do that, he told me, 'I just want to do this one right.' So when they started doing live shows again, I knew they were going to make it. Louis didn't have to do these shows from a financial standpoint. He was fine. I don't know if he knew all these measures were going to work, but he was going to try."

While the club was ready for a return to live comedy, there was just one more small detail: Lee needed comedians who were ready and willing to put on a show. "It was tough," Lee said. "A lot of comics weren't ready to start working again, and I completely understood that." One person who was ready was Greg Coleman.

Lee called Coleman immediately after hearing the news that the club could reopen and offered him the opportunity to be Acme's very first headliner of the pandemic era. "We had been hearing sprinkles of things like, 'Hey, this place and this place might open back up. It's going to look different, but they'll have people there,'" remembers Coleman. "As a comic, I'm like, *Heck yeah*. That's exciting to me. I was doing shows in parking lots, on the back of trucks, in my living room. So when Lou came to me and asked if I wanted the opportunity, I felt a big sense of responsibility."

While some were thrilled about the chance to leave their homes and get back to some semblance of live entertainment, others remained skeptical about whether the risk was worth the reward. "I felt a sense of social responsibility," Coleman continues. "The politics and social stuff really started cutting in, and people were like, 'How are you going to do a show and expose people?' I understood that, but also we were doing shows for adults who chose to take a calculated risk. The other thing I knew was that Acme was going to do whatever they needed to do in order to be in compliance. [Acme] reopening was a very artist-forward move. Louis could have washed his hands of the whole thing, but he wanted to make a commitment to try and get work for the comics, and to see if we could do it in a way that was sustainable. I think if it would have been horrible or a cover to be a money grab, he wouldn't have gone through with it. So when Lou brought it up to me, I said, 'Yeah man, I'm down to try.'"

On Saturday night, June 17, 2020, Acme officially reopened for business. And while there were plenty of people who were ready to laugh again, the crowd itself had a different feeling than before. "There was one audience, I think it was the Thursday show, and they just sucked," Coleman laughs. "They had this attitude like they were trying too hard to be woke. Like, 'You can't say that.' And I looked back at them like, 'I can and I did.' "

Given the climate of the world, especially locally in Minneapolis, over the past several months with the pandemic and the death of George Floyd and the subsequent fallout, it was unsurprising that Coleman would get onstage that week and discuss his experiences. "A lot of the feelings I had were still really fresh," he says. "It was an experience that I had personally, and of course everyone was going to have a take. There was such a temperature around the pandemic stuff and the George Floyd stuff, but that was stuff I had been talking about before anyways. It wasn't like police brutality was a thing where before [George Floyd] people were like, 'What? Does that happen?' Like we had been talking about it way before then. It might have felt weird for me if I didn't already talk about those things pre-pandemic, but that wasn't anything new."

Despite making a point to still be funny and not make the audience feel beaten down or lectured, Coleman says the pushback from that Thursday night audience was palpable. "They were feeling some type of way about the racial shit, but I told these jokes in Indiana and Wisconsin in some hard red spots, and those crowds were OK," he recalls. "My attitude was like, even if you feel uncomfortable, you need to hear it. And that's what I feel like talking about. And Louis had my back. He didn't want me to go into my bag and do old stuff. That's not why he hired me."

Though Coleman experienced a crowd that may have been overly sensitive, Bryan Miller noticed a very different energy when he performed for the pandemic-era audience. "I went to open mic night one of the first weeks it was back, and the

Greg Coleman had the honor of being the first headline act to perform at Acme after the club reopened. *Courtesy Greg Coleman*

whole tone was really different," Miller says. "It was really interesting. Jokes that would have gotten pushback from the Acme audience in the past were enthusiastically received by these people. And jokes that would have been enthusiastically received before were pushed back on."

While there were still plenty of people showing up because of their love of comedy, Miller says there was also a segment that showed up out of sheer defiance. "There was this energy like, 'I'm going to a comedy show because fuck the libs! They can't tell me where I can and can't go!' If it would have been like that at a Wisconsin bar show, I wouldn't have noticed. But at Acme, the crowd tends to be more metropolitan. So you could definitely feel the difference."

Despite the physical changes to the club, as well as the differences in clientele, Lee continued to operate the same way he always had. "Even with the reduced capacity, Louis was still paying comics the same rates [as he was pre-pandemic]," continues Miller. "The feature pay was still the same, and I remember being really grateful but also thinking, *How long can you afford to do this for, Louis?*" Paying the comics fairly wasn't the only thing Lee did during those limited-capacity shows that made little financial sense. But it all spoke to the spirit of the club.

That summer, the club once again hosted the Funniest Person Contest, with the winner still taking home a thousand-dollar grand prize. In the fall, the club hosted a show called "Recovery Riot," which was geared toward people in recovery from abuse of drugs and alcohol. The show was booze-free, thereby eliminating Lee's main source of income for the night, and proceeds benefited a local sober housing organization in St. Paul. Lee also put his new Zoom technology to good use, sharing the link for the show to all fifteen Hazelden addiction treatment facilities throughout the country, free of charge.

That November, immediately following the presidential election, Lee allowed Miller and Robert Baril to record an album at the club entitled *2020*, which featured each comic performing twenty minutes of material exclusively focused on the events of the past year. And much like the rest of 2020, it almost got shut down before it started. The week prior to Thanksgiving, positive COVID cases were on the rise, and local officials hoped to stop people from getting together too closely during the holiday break. Businesses were shut down once again, a decision that carried all the way into 2021. "We recorded the weekend before everything got shut down again," recalls Miller. "Like we made it by the skin of our teeth. We got through the late show Friday, and then everything had to close that night."

Despite the challenges and setbacks, Lee's dedication to using Acme to help develop talent, provide new opportunities, and grow his audience stayed as strong as ever. When the club was finally able to reopen in January, one of the very first weeks it was given an unexpected shot in the arm by an old friend.

Pete Lee, who by this time had become a favorite comic of *The Tonight Show Starring Jimmy Fallon*, was slated to appear on the show. However, Fallon wasn't having guests in studio just yet, so Pete and the producers arranged to record his *Tonight Show* set at Acme during his week at the club. "I was so happy to be able to do that for him," Pete beams. "Knowing everything he had gone through to keep the club open, and everything he had done for me personally, to hear Jimmy Fallon say, 'Live from Acme Comedy Company in Minneapolis,' was such a fitting tribute to him and the club."

Through the highs and lows of the lockdown and reopening, Acme continued to be a lighthouse breaking through the dark and uncertain waters of live entertainment. And while Lee may not have been sure what the future held for him and the club financially, he says it was the spirit of the comedians that kept him moving forward. "A lot of people were asking me if I thought comedy would ever come back," Lee says. "And I remember one of the first weeks after we reopened, I was at the club for the open mic, and it was full. The open mic people never quit. That's when I knew it would come back. The audience side would work itself out eventually. As long as there were still a bunch of creative people who wanted to do comedy, it would be OK."

As spring arrived and vaccines were rolled out to the public, Lee and the management team were forced to take on the challenges of checking vaccine cards, and to deal with the fallout from both sides of the argument. "The vax cards were the worst," remembers Rhodes. "We'd get emails from people being super yes or super no about what we're doing. No matter what we did, it was like, 'I supported your business during the pandemic and you're not doing things the way I want.'"

"It was so frustrating," Simon adds. "And it was so hard

because it was such a weird gray area about what you should or shouldn't do." No matter how challenging things got, however, Lee remained dedicated. "I reminded myself that this was the same thing I went through in 1991 when we first opened," he recalls. "I knew that the doors could close at any time. But at least this time it wouldn't be because I couldn't pay the bills."

Finally, that May, more than a year after Acme had hosted its last live show with a sellout audience, the announcement was made that businesses could once again operate at full capacity. "I remember I got kind of teary-eyed when we first put all the chairs back in the club," says Rhodes. "It was like, 'Oh that's right. *This* is what the club is really like.' I remember

No matter who is standing on the stage or holding the microphone, Acme will always belong to the comics. *Courtesy Brandon Simon*

I had servers coming up to me the night we reopened who hadn't been there before the pandemic, and [they] said, like, 'There are too many chairs in the club.' And it was just sort of like, no that's how it's supposed to be."

Over the coming months, things would settle into a new normal. Open mic night would move from Mondays to Tuesdays. Weekend shows started an hour earlier, at 7 P.M. and 9:30 P.M., which was a holdover from the city-imposed curfews months prior. And of course, new emcees were hired to work in the club, while existing Acme talent made the leap to feature and headliner status. "The pandemic created a lot of opportunities for comics," Coleman reflects. "A lot of people who were really good took off and never came back, and that made room for a lot of new people who might not have had as much stage time available before the pandemic."

Most important, however, was the fact that after decades of tough challenges, unfair breaks, and confidence-rattling occurrences, Louis Lee proved to everyone that he wasn't a loser at all. He had created something that was larger than himself. Something more valuable than money. And something he had been chasing his entire life: a real home.

AFTERWORD

It's Tuesday night at Acme. Open mic night. Emma Dalenberg is sitting at a table in the bar, working on jokes she plans to test out later tonight during her five minutes onstage.

Dalenberg was born in 1999. Before she even entered the world, Louis Lee had nearly died in a car wreck, Dave Mordal had won the inaugural Funniest Person Contest, and Nick Swardson and Mitch Hedberg had become two of the biggest comics in the world, after cutting their teeth on the Acme stage. Before she was old enough to drive, Acme had already celebrated its twenty-year anniversary, and Louis Lee had brought Acme comedy back home to Hong Kong. And by the time she got hired as an emcee at Acme, the club had already survived a battle with the city, a tidal wave of negative press, and a global pandemic.

But right now, she isn't thinking about all the history that has happened inside this club. She's doing her best to come up with something unique and personal that she can talk about onstage, just as countless comics have done before her. "Once I got hired at Acme, I felt like I could be more free onstage," Dalenberg says. "Comics who work at Acme tell you that once you're there, you've earned that freedom. The club wants you to try shit, to bomb, to do whatever. Having that freedom to really try stuff, and having a club where the ownership wants comedy to get better and understands that failure is a part of that process, it's just a really great feeling that no one can take away from me."

Growing up, Dalenberg wasn't aware of Acme or its long, storied history. But comedy did play an important role in her life. "When I was growing up, I'd listen to comedy with my dad when shit was really bad, and we'd laugh and it would make things feel brighter," she says. "Mitch Hedberg and Nick Swardson were two of my favorites. We loved listening to Tom Segura and Louis C. K. So when I first started coming to Acme and learned that all of those people had been important parts of that club, I was like, no fucking way. It was so exciting to realize all of that history was tied into one place."

Learning that history is important for comics like Dalenberg. Recognizing the talent that has left its mark on the club is inspiring for newbies considering getting onstage at Acme for the first time. And getting to see live comedy in such a well-respected and beloved venue is genuinely an honor for comedy fans.

But Louis Lee isn't worried about any of that right now. Instead, he's behind the bar helping the staff, serving drinks to customers, and sipping iced tea through a straw. It's rare to see a business owner who has had the longevity and success of Lee still getting his hands dirty—sometimes literally—while watching open mic sets to keep an eye on who might be the next comic to add their name to the famed wall of headliners hanging in the green room.

"Louis is an elusive guy," Dalenberg laughs when asked about her interactions with Lee. "He's been nice to me, though. He watched my set the first week I worked the club and told me I did a good job. But we didn't really have any in-depth conversation." Even after more than thirty years, Lee continues to carry on his reputation as a supportive but intimidating presence to new up-and-coming comics. But for those who have known him for years, the bond is stronger than ever.

In 2024, Lee suffered a medical emergency that nearly took his life. Believed to be caused by a complication from his accident decades earlier, a massive infection ripped through his body, nearly killing him. For the first time ever, comics had to reconcile what Acme might be like without Lee at the helm. "I worry about if and when Louis retires," says Jackie Kashian when asked about Acme's future. "Who has that energy and vision that he has? I really don't know."

And while the club itself is important for comics at any point in their career, whether they're longtime headliners like Kashian or scrappy newbies like Dalenberg working to prove themselves, the reality is that Acme is just a room with a stage. The true magic comes from the people who have stood on that stage, and the reputation the club has earned thanks to its unflinching dedication to the art of stand-up comedy. "I looked at Acme as the very top of what I thought was possible," Dalenberg continues. "Once I got hired at Acme I was like, *I did it*. I achieved my dream. Everything after this is just a bonus."

And as for Lee, who came to America as a teenage immigrant speaking no English, who lost all his family's money, and who nearly died while trying to keep the club open through personal, professional, and even global hardships, he's still as dedicated to helping the local comedy scene thrive as he was thirty years ago.

"I'm not saying I want to die before Louis," laughs Kashian, though her tone indicates she might not be joking. "Like, I can't tell him that he isn't allowed to retire until after I'm dead. And the thing is, even if Acme was gone, there will always be other work. I can make a room laugh, and I believe that is a skill I can apply anywhere. Acme itself means so much to me. But it's still just a place. It could close its doors forever tomorrow, and I would still go hang out with Louis at an old folks home. To me, Louis is Acme. And as long as he's around, I'll always have my home club."

ACKNOWLEDGMENTS

While telling the story of Acme Comedy Company and Louis Lee is a very big job, I didn't do it on my own. The story is made up of the people, moments, and, of course, the laughs that have happened inside that club. Thank you to Jim Meyer, Rich Miller, Jen Bryce, Tim Slagle, John DeBoer, C. Willi Myles, Jackie Kashian, Pete Lee, Chad Daniels, Tracey Ashley, Kevin Estling, T. J. Markwalter, J. Elvis Weinstein, Bryan Miller, Andy Erikson, K. P. Anderson, Robert Baril, Nate Abshire, Elaine Thompson, Sarah Drew, Mike Earley, Tim Harmston, Devohn Bland, Madeleine Farley, Greg Coleman, Nick Swardson, Maggie Faris, Emma Dalenberg, Brandon Simon, Hannah Rhodes, Joe Feely, and every single Acme comedian and audience member who has kept that room alive for more than three decades. Without you there is no Acme story. Thank you to my wife and kids for letting me run out to the comedy club on weeknights for "research." Thank you to my ex-wife for telling me "I think you should be a writer instead" when I told her I wanted to try being a stand-up comedian.

But most importantly, thank you, Louis. Not just for everything you do for comedy, for the comics, and for me personally, but for being a friend.

SELECTED BIBLIOGRAPHY

Chapter 3

"Funny Thing About Minnesota: A Woman's Place Is in the (Virtual) Spotlight." Zoom book event, March 30, 2021. Minnesota Historical Society. YouTube. https://www.youtube.com/watch?v=IvAtwvTzyso.

Strait, Patrick. "Acme Comedy Company at 30." *Racket*, November 3, 2021.

Chapter 4

Covert, Colin. "The Last Laughs at the Comedy Gallery." Minneapolis *Star Tribune*, August 1, 1996.

Chapter 8

The Funniest Person Podcast. Acme Comedy Company. YouTube.

Chapter 11

I Need You to Kill. Documentary, 2017. Directed by J. Elvis Weinstein.

Chapter 12

Roper, Eric. "Not Kidding: Threat to Acme Comedy Brings Crowd to City Hall." Minneapolis *Star Tribune*, June 28, 2016.

Chapter 13

Interview with Louis C. K. *The Tonight Show with Jimmy Fallon*. April 7, 2015.

Shortal, Jana. "Acme Comedy Is Giving Louis C.K. the Stage This Week, and Jana Sat Down with the Owner to Talk about Why." *KARE 11*, May 9, 2019.

INDEX

Page numbers in *italics* refer to illustrations.
"Lee" in subentries refers to Louis Lee.

ABOUT THE AUTHOR

Patrick Strait has been writing about stand-up comedy in the Twin Cities for nearly two decades. Whether it's exploring the history of Minnesota stand-up through his book, *Funny Thing About Minnesota . . .*, or spotlighting comedians who are making an impact on the comedy scene today through publications like *Racket*, *City Pages*, *The Growler*, Thrillist, Dispatch, and others, he focuses on what makes stand-up such an incredible art form and the people who have taken it to new heights. He himself is moderately funny at best.